THE BITTER TASTE OF DYING

A Memoir

JASON SMITH

Thought Catalog Books
Brooklyn, NY

Written for Jaden and Isabella.

Dedicated to Uncle Mark, Aunt Laurelle, and the millions of others lost to this addiction thing. You are missed.

CONTENTS

vii

Some names and identifying details have been changed to protect the privacy of individuals

PROLOGUE

"I'm not really sure what you want me to say," I told him.

He looked annoyed. "Alright, well how about this," he said, unimpressed. "How about you get the fuck out of my house and come back when you're ready to try things my way." He stood up, ready to usher me from his deck to my car.

Decision time. This guy was my "sponsor." I was a "drug addict." All I knew was I wanted to stop "doing drugs" because my life had "gone to shit," but I didn't know how. I had shredded my life into pieces, pushing away anyone I'd ever been close with. Friends. Family. Acquaintances. I had nobody.

No job. No money. Nothing.

Two months earlier I overdosed on Thanksgiving, in front of my dad, sister, nephew. In front of my 1 year old son. When I woke up in the hospital, I made a decision: The world would be a better place without me in it.

The only thing sadder than that decision itself was how easy it was to come to.

I couldn't live my life doing drugs because my body was beginning to degenerate from years of substance abuse and overdoses were becoming more and more frequent. Counting overdoses where I ended up in the hospital, I was at 6. Overdoses where I woke up covered in vomit, alone, wondering how I didn't choke in my sleep – there were too many to count. I was a walking, textbook-definition of drug addict. But I couldn't live my life without drugs either. I'd tried that and was miserable.

There's a line in the song "Down in a Hole" by Alice in Chains that goes:

"I've eaten the sun / so my tongue has been burned of the taste."

I'm not sure there's a better description of trying to get clean. When you experience pure bliss in its most euphoric form, plain old reality is shitty. Your average, everyday life is pretty fucking boring and doesn't provide the exciting, seductive, quasi-orgasmic feeling you get from the drugs. I'd tried getting clean and I hated every second of it, which left me in a pretty horrible situation: I couldn't live with the drugs, and I couldn't live without them.

So I decided living just wasn't for me.

I tried taking my own life on November 29, 2012. It's ironic that my attempt occurred in a dark, damp, filthy apartment, completely alone in my isolation and depression. The drugs didn't always affect me in this way.

When I first started using, the drugs made me social, comfortable, talkative and friendly. The life of the party. I had the confidence to talk to that girl I could never talk to before. I became a social centerpiece at bars and parties. While everyone else was partaking in socially acceptable drugs like alcohol, I drank a cherry Coke, high and happy.

Fast forward 16 years, and everything the drugs gave me in the beginning, they took away. That comfortable, confident, social person was now insecure in isolation, alone, depressed, so uncomfortable in his own skin that he was going to kill himself.

Worse, everything the drugs took away in the beginning they brought back tenfold. The demons, the pain, the hurt, the insecurities were now enhanced, more so than before the drugs entered my life. Add to that all of the guilt and shame I acquired from doing the dirty, conniving, manipulative shit one must do to maintain a healthy drug habit, and you find yourself on a couch, ready to die.

It's depressing to wake up from a suicide attempt and realize, "Shit, I can't even do THAT right." My suicide attempt failed, leaving me to wake up in a bathtub of blood and warm water.

I couldn't live with drugs. I couldn't live without drugs. And now I couldn't even die.

A year earlier I came across this guy who'd eventually become my sponsor. I heard he went to 12-step meetings and had gotten his life together, and I kept his phone number just in case I ever made the decision to do the same. With nowhere else to go, no one else to call, no move left to make – I reached for my phone and called him.

I wasn't even sure what a sponsor was, but this guy was the only person who seemed to want me around. Every 12-step meeting I went to, all I heard was, "Get a sponsor," or, "Have you gotten a sponsor yet?" So I found this guy just to shut them up. We'd sat before and talked about my past, but nothing too in-depth. This time was different.

I was supposed to be completely open and honest with him, something at which I was struggling mightily. Shit, I wasn't even sure where to start.

"Is this, like, some kind of confession or something," I asked him.

"No," he replied. "You got some shit inside of you that you need to get out."

"Why should I tell you?" I asked suspiciously.

"Because if you don't, there's a good chance you're going to die."

He was right. It was a miracle I wasn't dead already.

"Look, man," he said, "I'm here to help you because I've been through it. Everything you've done, I've done. Anything you've thought, I've thought. Give it a shot, and if it doesn't work, you can get a full refund on the misery and depravity your life has become."

I looked at him. Once upon a time, he did 4 years in Folsom Prison on drug and drug-related charges. He was what I was: A guy who couldn't stop doing drugs, despite his life being destroyed from the inside out. He'd been to the same hell I'd been to, souvenir-scars and all. Our stories matched, but only the first half. He made it out. He made something of his life. He took his second chance and made the most of it. This guy owned a business, had a good looking wife and adorable kids. He was a productive member of society. I wanted what he had because I wanted to be what he was.

"Ok, so what do we do?" I asked.

"Why don't you start from the beginning," he said. "You said something about your uncle...?"

CHAPTER 1.

THE BITTER TASTE OF DYING

Fourteen years old is far too young to find out what death tastes like, but I remember it.

Vividly.

In case you're wondering, it tastes bitter—although when giving mouth-to-mouth resuscitation to a dying man whose body's last gasp is foaming at the mouth, it's hard to differentiate between the taste and the smell and the visual. It, like the memory, just sort of all blends together.

Regardless, it was far too young. I was far too young.

Remember when they told us that a brain on drugs looks like a frying egg? I can tell you first hand, that's not what it looks like. It's far more disturbing than that. It's much more grotesque.

My uncle Mark was a good man. He really was. He had a great heart, an infectious laugh, and used to pull these girls who were insanely beautiful. Just gorgeous. Growing up, I admired him. I wanted to be him.

I loved him so much.

It really is a shame that the last image of him I have is of him dying, lying on the floor, my left hand behind his head, my right hand under his chin, trying to somehow exhale my life into his. Syringe to his right, burnt spoon on the table, empty saran wrap and lighter on the floor.

Just absolute chaos.

Part of me feels like Mark deserves a better final mental snapshot than that.

But then again, heroin is an evil drug.

There will always be questions about that day that I'll never get answers to. Like where he got the heroin, since he had no car, no money, and we lived in the middle of nowhere.

Or whether his feeble attempt at staying clean by "white knuckling" it drove him to the point where he decided to just end it all that morning, before I got out of bed, not really giving a shit that a 14-year-old kid would be the one to find him.

I guess I'll never really know.

It was the summer of 1994. O.J. Simpson had just killed his wife, Bill Clinton was accused of sexual harassment — again. I was out of school for the next few months so I didn't really give a shit about any of it.

My family had recently come into a little bit of money and bought a piece of land in a small housing development that was about three miles from civilization. The land they bought used to be the community swimming pool and pool house, so needless to say the neighbors were not exactly thrilled with our arrival.

We took their pool and pool house. I'd have been pissed too.

The day I found out we were moving my dad called me into the living room.

"Jas," he explained. "I'm gonna need you and your friends to build a house this summer."

Huh? I don't know anything about building a house.

"Let them know I'll pay them."

Note, he wasn't asking. He was telling. Also note, he said pay *them*.

I was just an indentured servant.

But that's my dad. He's well known to come up with these off-the-wall, bat shit crazy ideas, 99.9% of which never comes to fruition. He's an idea guy, but when it comes to actually implementing the idea, there is some sort of mental disconnect.

This just happened to fall into that .1%. My friends and I were actually going to build a house.

We moved all of our things into the pool house, converted one of the bathrooms into a kitchen, knocked out a wall, and turned it into a little studio apartment.

I got my own little trailer on the property, alongside the swimming pool fence, which gave me the privacy that a 14-year-old boy just needs.

Thankfully, my friends and I were not going to be doing this alone. We were bringing in a contractor. A foreman. Someone with construction experience, who would show my friends and me what the hell we were doing and hopefully keep the occupational hazards to a minimum.

Uncle Mark.

My favorite uncle. He still had the handlebar mustache that I remembered as a kid, but by now he was missing a few teeth, and had this sort of heroin chic, rock star figure. It was obvious that either the years or the drugs were beginning to take their toll on him.

It was probably both.

My uncle Mark was an anomaly. He was a heroin addict, but had never been to jail, unless you count a short stint in the same Tijuana jail cell to which I'd eventually pay a visit myself.

Family traditions, you know?

The first time my uncle shot heroin was in a park in San Diego sometime around 1970. Heroin was getting pretty big in the early 70s, with a bunch of Vietnam vets coming home with vicious habits that they'd developed while stationed in the Golden Triangle. Shit, I'd probably shoot up too if my reality consisted of jungles, monsoons, and bullets. With such a demand returning stateside, it wasn't long before the supply end of things caught up here at home.

Economics 101.

For a future junkie, it was the right place at the right time, and for Mark, it was that park on that day.

Someone in the park hit him and his friend up, asking if they wanted to give it a try (I might note here, that "someone" eventually became a lawyer, whose personal guilt for turning so many people onto such an evil drug led him to represent anyone he'd ever sold to for free).

How generous of him.

Anyway, the future litigator sold Mark and his friend a bag of dope, and they shot it up.

Instant Euphoria.

I know my uncle had a pretty fucked up childhood, so I can only imagine the relief he must have felt when he was able to numb those demons that first time.

Unbeknownst to Mark, the chase had begun, from zero to forever with a single shot to the vein. It would never be the same after that. Ever.

"What was it like?" I asked Mark's accomplice from the park on the day of Mark's funeral. "Like, what did it feel like?"

"It felt so good, so incredible, so out-of-this-world fucking orgasmic," he explained, "that it scared me from ever touching the drug again. It felt that good."

"What about Mark?" I asked, already knowing the answer.

"He felt the exact same way—except he wanted to feel that way forever. He wanted that feeling every day for the rest of his life."

He was 14 years old.

Mark always worked, always had a job. Total functioning addict. He worked construction, but was not a "construction worker." Mark was a carpenter. His craft was truly something amazing, and the things he could do with a hammer, a level, and a few nails were magical.

He worked every day to support his habit and was pretty built because of it. But he'd also worked his way through all of those beautiful girlfriends I remembered as a kid. All of them were clean, "normies," all wanting to fix him. Save him. Each knew the previous girl had failed, but they were different. A few of them paid for him to go to rehab. It never took. He even once had a girl who came from some serious money, who told him if he went to Hawaii, to some movie-star rehab and stayed clean for a year, she'd pay him a million dollars. Honest to God! And he chose the needle over the money.

Heroin, boy. It's a motherfucker.

He used to shoot up in the veins of his feet, so he wouldn't have track marks in his arms. In Southern California at this time, if the police saw that you had track marks, they could take you in and book you. No questions asked. So he hid them by shooting up in his feet.

And occasionally in his neck if the occasion called for flip-flops.

For 25 years he'd carried on this way, working and spending his paycheck on heroin.

Every. Single. Day.

He'd finally reached that point in his life where the girlfriends could never get him to stop. He wanted to stop. He wanted to be done. For himself. No million dollar prize, no potential wife, no nothing on the other end. He finally wanted to quit for himself.

So he called my dad and asked if he could come up and get clean. My dad, being the resourceful idealist he is, figured he'd kill two birds with one stone—have his heroin addict brother teach my friends and me how to build a house.

By this time, most of the family had given up on Mark. Chalked him up as a lost cause. But not my dad. My father welcomed his little brother up to Auburn with open arms, and boy—did my uncle ever make a grand appearance. He arrived high as a fucking kite. Smiling his ass off, eyelids set to sunset, not a care in the world. He got that last fix, that last taste of seduction, that last blanket of warmth, and his first night up he began nodding off in the middle of dinner.

That's right. That's the uncle Mark I remember. Cool as shit.

That summer is forever burned into my memory. My dad drove a tow truck, and my uncle Mark went with him every day. My dad wouldn't let him out of his sight. He forced Mark to go to AA meetings each day, but my uncle didn't like it.

My dad did not care. Whether he liked it or not, Mark

was going to go to meetings. It was a combination of family rehab and Prop. 36, before Prop 36 existed.

Mark got clean. For a little while, at least.

My routine that summer involved leaving in the morning for football practice, practicing, and coming home to work on the house. Not knowing it at the time, I'd met my new best friend through football, Mikey, who basically started living at my house. Mikey was "good people." A solid friend, but always without a ride. Always. When he got dropped off at my house, I think his mom just forgot about him, because he never left. He'd catch a ride home from time to time to grab clothes and video games, and then he'd be back. When my parents gave me money for lunch, they gave Mikey money for lunch. When they gave me money to go to a Homecoming dance, they gave Mikey money for the dance.

He and I became inseparable.

I watched my uncle kick a little bit, but I think he went through the worst of it while he was with my dad. Driving around Sacramento in the middle of the summer picking up and dropping off cars wasn't, I'm sure, his ideal place to go through heroin withdrawal. At the time I did not understand it, but looking back now, I have crazy respect for him being able to kick in this fashion. I know it must have been anything but easy.

After about 10 days, he started coming to life. He'd get home with my dad, take his shirt off and just jump in the pool, jeans and all. Perhaps it was his own way of trying to recover, a little self-baptism. He did it every day and emerged from the water with a smile on his face. Then he'd go to his trailer, change pants, light up a Marlboro Red, and socialize.

He hung out with Mikey and me a lot. Emotionally, my

uncle was about 14, the same age that we were. Like a kid with a fake ID. And facial hair.

We would laugh, listen to music, and just bond. Mark was an incredible ping-pong player. I guess all those rehabs did serve a purpose. Just not the intended one. My dad bought us a ping-pong table, and we would play for hours. Epic battles to 21. Neither Mikey nor myself could beat Mark, but we got very good at ping-pong ourselves. We had to. Mark could literally injure you during a ping-pong match if you didn't bring it.

Swear to God.

Mikey and I are both hyper-competitive and despise losing, and there were many nights we cussed each other out and went to bed swearing we'd never talk again because of some controversial ping-pong decision.

"Fuck you, man, that hit the table. You know it. Fuck it, I'm going home tomorrow. You can build your house by yourself, asshole."

I knew he wasn't going to really go home. He didn't have a ride.

We'd wake up the next morning as if nothing happened and just go on with our day. That's the beauty of youth. Resentments don't really stick.

As the summer rolled on, I got to really know my uncle well. I got to know the real him. The clean him. The him that all of his girlfriends, all of his friends, everyone who entered his life after that fateful day in the park wanted so badly to find. He was a beautiful human being. He was loving, nurturing, and a really funny guy. He had an incautious laugh, and when he got out of that tow truck each day, before jumping in the pool, he'd yell out to me, "What is up, Jason!" Exactly like he used to do when I was little.

I loved it. For that summer, he was my other new best friend.

He pulled together a few months clean, and my parents must have really thought he'd finally gotten it. Since we lived out in the country and he had no car, my uncle was pretty much stranded on our little compound.

He didn't know anybody in Auburn, didn't know where to buy, who to call, who to contact. He was clean whether he wanted to stay that way or not.

He was safe. There was no way he was going to find dope—not where we lived. No way. Not in a new town that was about 400 miles from any dealer he knew.

Underestimating the ingenuity of a drug addict—that was the one mistake my parents made.

Before my uncle's arrival, my mom's parents had made plans for my mom and dad to fly down to Las Vegas for a weekend in late August. My parents had forgotten all about it when my grandmother called a week before the trip to serve a friendly reminder.

My mom tried to explain, "I'm sorry, but I don't think we can make it. Bruce's brother Mark is staying with us and he's only a few months clean, and I'm not sure I trust…"

My grandmother, being the compassionate soul she is, interrupted. "Mark? I thought for sure he'd be dead by now."

For whatever reason my mom bit, after what I'm sure was a hefty guilt trip. She and my dad rationalized their way into a weekend in Vegas, but not before laying down some ground rules:

No drugs.

No friends with cars.

No parties.

No girls.

And those were just for Mark.

As for Mikey and me, they told us to be good and keep an eye on him. At 14 years old, I was left in charge for the weekend.

They left on a Friday. I went to football practice that morning, preparing for a scrimmage that we were playing in Rio Linda the following day. I was excited. My uncle heard that I was a good football player, but had never seen me play. I was prepared to put on a show for him.

Finally, he'd get to see one of my games.

After practice that Friday, Mikey, Mark and I had ourselves a proper Friday night. Mark threw on a Jimi Hendrix record, "Hey Joe" blasting out of the house speakers. We played ping-pong, we swam, we laughed, we joked, we teased. It was great. Mark and I started a ping-pong match, and for the first time, I was hanging with him. When you played Mark, you had to play a defensive game, standing about 3 feet back from your end of the table. You had to play every shot perfectly or he was going to leave little ping-pong ball-sized bruises all across your chest.

We played to 21, all tied up, and you had to win by 2. Eventually the score was 33-32, my lead, him serving.

I anticipated his serve, hit a shot that ricocheted off his end of the table and redirected straight down, not allowing him to hit a return.

I'd done it. I beat Mark in ping-pong.

I was ecstatic. I began looking around for cameras to tell that I was going to Disney World, circling the pool with my arms outstretched as if I was set for takeoff, emitting a sound that was somewhere between a laugh and a scream.

I was all smiles, and so was Mark. He had a unique look in his eyes when I beat him. If I didn't know any better, I'd say he was proud of me. We shook hands after the game was over and went on with our night.

If I'd only known that was the last night I would ever spend with him, I might have let it soak in a little bit more.

Around midnight, Mikey and I were getting tired. Mark had found some vodka from somewhere, and was mixing screwdrivers.

I swear to God, I had no idea what he was preparing to do that night.

Mikey and I went to sleep, and Mark said he was going to stay up a little longer. I told him I'd see him in the morning. I never even hugged him goodbye.

The next morning I woke up like any other morning, leaving Mikey asleep on the top bunk. I walked out of the trailer, hung a right into the gate surrounding the swimming pool, and made my way into the pool house. When I walked through the door, my heart dropped down to my stomach.

Sitting on the couch was Mark, leaned back, left arm out, head back. I saw the needle sitting there, still in his arm. The table was cluttered with matches, a lighter, a blackened spoon, and a little, empty plastic baggy. His eyes were closed, but he was breathing. His breaths were spaced out, but deep. He was breathing out of his mouth.

I froze.

I didn't know what to do. I was afraid to call 911 because I didn't want him to get in trouble. I didn't yet know what a normal heroin high looked like. I figured this was it-- that he'd wake up and be embarrassed, beg me to not tell my parents, and we'd move on.

But there was also a part of me that was afraid he was

dying. That told me to call 911. That told me it would save his life. Yet I did nothing.

I didn't want to wake Mikey up, because this was MY uncle. I didn't want Mikey to know. I was ashamed. My uncle lay dying on the couch, and I was ashamed of him.

After weighing my options, I decided to pull up a chair and watch. Front row seat. I grabbed a kitchen chair, placed it directly in front of Mark, and just watched him.

For about an hour, nothing changed. His breathing stayed the same. Every once in a while he'd twitch and one of those twitches caused the syringe to fall out of his arm, onto the couch. I picked it up and held it in my hands. I looked at it. It was empty. There was a little bit of blood on the tip of the needle, and it felt strange in my hands but I was also a bit fascinated by it, in a morbid way. I eventually put it on the table, next to the burnt spoon. It was about this time that Mark's breathing changed.

Instead of evenly spaced out deep breaths, his chest shot out, like he was trying to push it out as far as he could. His chest was so far out, his back was arched and inverted. Eyes still closed, his chest would go out, and then suck in just as far as before, but the opposite direction.

Then nothing. No breathing, no nothing. Seconds passed. They seemed agonizingly long.

Then, without notice, suddenly, his chest shot back out. Then back in, same as before. This went on for about a half hour, and I just watched. I didn't call 911. I didn't wake Mikey. I just sat there. Watching.

Chest out.

Chest in.

As I watched, I looked at his face, noticing the lines. The scars of aging. I was so scared, but I didn't know what to do. I didn't want my uncle to be arrested. I didn't want to call 911, have police show up, just to have him wake up and look at me like I was some kind of snitch. But I didn't know how to help.

Again, I just froze.

I heard Mikey wake up, and I walked outside to tell him what had happened, so he wouldn't just stumble onto the scene like I did.

"I think Mark is dying," was all I could say.

Those weren't the intended words, but those are the words that came out.

When Mikey and I walked in together, Mark all of a sudden stopped breathing. Completely. I knew he wasn't going to start again, because he started oozing a yellow something out of his mouth and his nose. Because he had a handlebar mustache, all that yellow shit was covering his mustache.

I felt disgusted at the site, and then disgusted with myself for feeling that way. For the rest of the day, this is what I went through. I'd feel something, from the very core of my human condition, and then be ashamed for feeling it.

That was a microcosm for how I'd spend the next twenty years when thinking about this whole fucking chaotic day.

I finally called 911, and the operator on the phone was a total bitch.

"I need an ambulance. I think my uncle overdosed on heroin."

"Ok, sir. What time did you guys last use the drug?" *You guys? How the fuck did I get dragged into this?*

"Umm… We didn't use the drug. He did. And I don't

know, because I woke up and just found him slumped back on the couch."

"Ok, well why do you think he's overdosed?"

"Because HE'S FUCKING DYING, SO CAN YOU PLEASE SEND HELP?"

"Ok, sir, no need to yell. Do you at least know CPR?"

Really, lady? You're going to choose NOW to be condescending?

My whole insides were just tumbling around my stomach in a way I'd never felt before. I just wanted to run away and find a spot where none of this shit was real.

"I took CPR in 8th grade, but I'm not sure I remember it."

She sounded like she was getting annoyed with me now. "Ok, well, if he is not breathing you need to give him mouth-to-mouth. And if he has no pulse, you will need to give chest compressions."

I put the phone down. I didn't need to hear her anymore.

I pinched his nose, pulled his chin up, and put my mouth onto his. It was a strange, strange sensation. So much different than those plastic dummies we practiced on in 8th grade.

This was a real human fucking being.

His skin was warm. There was yellow shit coming out of his mouth and nose, and it was getting inside of mine, starting to coat the insides of my cheek. I could feel it on the back of my throat. His head was heavier than I anticipated.

That taste is unforgettable. Death tastes bitter, with a texture that falls somewhere between gritty and horrific, staining the memory for good. There's no going back from it. Once there, it remains. Forever. All the therapy in the world can't erase it.

This was my uncle. My friend. Dying in my arms.

I pressed my mouth against his, fighting the gag reflex I felt coming as I felt that yellow shit on the back of my tongue, and tried blowing air into his lungs, but I could tell no air was getting through. Whatever was coming out of his mouth was blocking his air passage. I tried putting my finger inside to scoop it out, but couldn't. When I pulled out yellow shit, more just took its place. Mikey began pumping on his chest, but I knew it was over. Mikey tried to give him mouth-to-mouth as well, with me pumping on Mark's chest, as if we were the problem.

And it was at this time, for whatever reason, that my brain threw me a curve ball.

I started laughing. Hysterically. For a few seconds, all I could do was laugh. It was crazy. The laughter came from somewhere deep inside me that I didn't know existed, and I couldn't stop it. Perhaps it was the absurdity of the situation, or maybe it was a subconscious defense mechanism. I don't know. But there was my dying uncle, and I sat there, with yellow shit all over my mouth, laughing like some kind of fucking maniac.

When the paramedics showed up, they arrived in two ambulances, followed by a gang of Placer County Sheriffs. I don't remember much from then on. I don't remember talking to the police. I don't remember talking to the paramedics. I don't remember anything. I remember someone asking for a phone number to contact my parents, and I told them I didn't have one.

"They're in Las Vegas. That's all I know."

But I lied. That wasn't all I knew. I knew that my uncle was dead, and it was my fault. I knew that had I called 911 sooner, right when I found him, he'd be alive. I knew

I laughed while he died, and I hated myself for it. I knew what death tasted like. I also knew that my life had changed. I didn't yet know what direction it would take, but I knew it would be a much darker one.

The second paramedic that stayed behind to talk to us pulled me aside a few minutes after they took Uncle Mark away. He wanted to tell me that my uncle had "expired." And that it had happened between our house and the hospital. But I knew he was lying. He didn't want me to know that my uncle died in front of me. But I already knew. I was there. I still had yellow crust around my lips from trying to give him CPR. I'd felt his pulse. There was none.

"You should always remember, that you were there to watch his last breath."

This fucking guy actually told me that. As if that was some sort of honor bestowed upon me.

Truth is, his last breath was the one I was unable to get into his lungs. That's how I saw it, at least.

The rest of the day is a blur. But I know that I never cried. It was as if that crazy, chaotic, morbid scene that I'd just been through had never happened.

In fact, I played in my football game that night. The Varsity coach, Coach Von Housen, pulled me aside and told me he'd heard about my uncle and that he was sorry.

"It's nothing, Coach. I'm good."

And I meant it. I took all of the guilt, all of the shame, the confusion, the hurt, the pain that I felt about that whole fucking fiasco that I'd just endured, and just stuffed it inside. I wouldn't deal with it, in a healthy way, for another twenty years.

But at that moment I was a football player. Saturated in misidentified emotion, lost but sincerely trying, I moved forward because I wasn't sure what in the hell else I was supposed to do. Or where in the hell else I was supposed to go.

For that night, I was a football player because, quite frankly, being anything other than that hurt too goddamn much.

I had no idea that that night would be the first of a twenty-year journey where I'd learn to do any and everything to keep from ever feeling just exactly what that hurt felt like.

"Damn, that's pretty fucked up," said my sponsor. "That must have been hard."

"Yeah, but I got through it," I told him.

I'd told this story to quite a few people through the years, with the same bullshit reply to their "That must have been hard" statement. "Yeah, but I got through it." And every time, they commended me for being so strong, for taking such a traumatic experience and persevering. In fact, there's a part of me that used that story to get that response, because I was so insecure, I needed their approval, even if it meant manipulating them by recounting the story of my dead uncle. I expected his response to be the same.

"Bullshit," he said, bluntly, catching me by surprise. "You didn't get through it. You just stuffed it down. If you'd 'gotten through it,' you wouldn't be sitting here with me now, needing my help to stop doing drugs."

He had a point.

"It's time you man up and really take a look at how you, as a person, changed after that."

I thought about this. "I mean, of course it changed me. How could it not?"

"Ok," he said, seeing this was finally going somewhere, "how did you feel after that? Did you hate him for overdosing? Did you hate yourself for not saving him? Did you hate your parents for leaving you alone?"

"Actually, I just played football. When I was playing, my mind was occupied. Football sort of protected my thoughts from Mark's death."

"I'm just curious," my sponsor asked me, "how did football become such a source of refuge for you?"

I laughed. "That's sort of an interesting story..."

CHAPTER 2.

THANK GOD FOR DRIVE-BY SHOOTINGS

He told me we were going to the store. That was the plan.

But he had a certain pep in his step that I wasn't used to seeing, and my seven-year-old instincts told me that my dad was up to something.

"Jas," he exclaimed, grinning from ear-to-ear. "Put your shoes on! We're going to the store!"

He said it with such excitement, such anticipation. I put my shoes on, got into his old primer-colored El Camino, and set out with him for "the store."

We passed the store. Just drove right by it like it wasn't there.

Then we passed the second store, which just looked at us as we drove by, as if it, too, were wondering what my dad was up to.

My dad, God bless him, just kept driving, heavily-distorted oldies pushing the limits of his stock Chevy speakers, as if nothing was going down.

We got onto the freeway driving toward an area I'd never been before. To adults it was known as Southeast San Diego, but to me it was just a place where all the kids were black.

Finally we arrived to the Skyline neighborhood, where we were the only two white people on the entire block. I was used to diversity, but this was minority status. And we were the minorities.

The sun was setting and about half of the streetlights came on. I suppose the other half quit on the job, seeing no point in illuminating such dilapidated housing.

We pulled into the Morse High School parking lot where, upon seeing us, one of the lot's inhabitants asked out loud, "Who the fuck is this white boy?"

I wasn't sure which person said it because they were in a group. And I wasn't sure if he was talking about my dad or me. But I was pretty sure that it didn't matter because somebody wanted to know "who the fuck" we were.

My dad got out of the car and looked around, surveying the scene. I just sat and waited, door locked, seatbelt on, looking straight ahead and still wondering what in the hell my dad was up to. As he closed the door to the El Camino, he looked at the group and I could see that he was about to say something.

Oh dear God, dad, no.

He looked at them with a big old grin, long hair blowing in the breeze, beard hanging off of his face, wearing a fucking Hawaiian shirt of all things, and yelled out, in his urban voice, "What's up HOMEBOYS?"

Oh my God, Dad.

Silence. Uncomfortable, awkward silence. More silence.

I don't think they knew how to respond. Perhaps it was shock, or confusion, or respect for the balls that it took to just say what he said and how he said it, but in unison they all cracked up laughing. One of them came over to my dad and shook his hand.

"You're alright, man," he said, chuckling. "You're alright."

My dad just stood there, chest out, still smiling, as if to say, "Yeah, I know."

Then he shifted focus. "Jas, hop out of the car!" I did as he asked after unlocking the door, and then taking off my seatbelt. I could feel everybody watching me. He pulled a pair of used, black MacGregor cleats out from under the El Camino's bench seat.

"Here, Jason, put these on. They're like regular shoes but they make it so you don't slip when you run on the grass."

The grass? What grass? Why will I be running on grass?

As I sat in the car putting on the shoes, my dad put his hand on my cheek. "OK, now Jas, you're going to play football," he said, eyes opened wide with excitement. "You're gonna be a football player! Now run out there."

Wait... what? Football? Don't I have any say in this? What happened to going to the store?

Then the group in the parking lot joined in. "Run out there, Jas!" they hollered, half-mockingly, half-sincere. "They need a white boy on their team!"

The whole group laughed.

I did not.

I was seven-years-old, blonde hair that covered my eyes and my ears, having never even thrown a football, running onto a field to join a team of kids that were bigger than me, older than me, and a lot fucking blacker than me. I was scared to death.

One of the coaches saw me from a distance and smiled: "You must be Jason," he yelled out.

I wonder what gave it away.

"Come over here and give me twenty push ups," he

barked, feigning annoyance like adults do when they're not really mad but want kids to think they are. "You're late." I struggled through three push ups, which were all my scrawny arms could muster at that point in life.

Getting up, I lied and told him I was finished. "OK, now run over there to Coach Kurtis. He's gonna get you some pads and a helmet."

This was football's Golden Age. Coaches punished players by withholding water breaks. If you had signs of a concussion, coaches slapped you on the side of the helmet until you told him they were gone. If a coach cussed you out during practice, parents didn't get involved. They didn't file lawsuits. In fact, you probably got an ass whooping once you got home for doing whatever made the coach cuss you out in the first place. If you were hurt, you toughed it out. If you were injured, you still practiced. Just with a limp.

And if a kid whose dad tricked him into joining your team showed up late to practice a few weeks into the season, you simply gave him pads and a helmet on his first day.

That first practice was brutally painful. Off to the sideline Coach Kurtis fit me into some shoulder pads, a number 77 jersey, pants, and a helmet that was way too big for me. Slapping me on the side of the helmet, he knelt down until we were eye-level, gold chain around his neck, and just looked at me. He stared into my eyes as if he were trying to read something. All I saw in his eyes was sympathy.

Standing up he yelled out, "OK, Smith, run back over to Coach Layne." Guessing Coach Layne was the guy I just lied to about my push-ups, I did as I was told, all the while still wondering what in the hell was going on.

The helmet was heavy and the shoulder pads felt strange. I ran halfway to Coach Layne, about forty yards, and started walking because I was winded. I'd never played any sport and was in the shape of a seven-year-old who watched a lot of cartoons.

This caught Coach Layne's attention and he did not look happy. "Smith! What in the hell are you doing walking on MY field?" He was stomping in my direction taking big, long strides. "We don't walk on this field, we run! Do you understand me?"

"Yes," I said, still trying to catch my breath.

"Yes WHAT?" He was getting more pissed.

I wasn't sure what to say, so I said nothing.

"YES, WHAT?"

I stood there just looking at him, confused, wishing we'd just gone to the fucking grocery store.

"Smith, you address every coach on this field with 'Yes, sir,' do you understand me?"

The whole team was looking at me. Silently.

As I began running, I blurted out, "Yes."

"Yes? Smith, what in the hell is wrong with you? Hey, Coach Kurtis! I think Smith is a little slow!"

"Yes, sir," I said, finally catching on.

"There you go, Smith," he said, finally satisfied, smiling. "Now come on. You're just in time for angle drills."

Angle drills?

Now for those who were raised in a more nurturing environment, let me explain. In angle drills, the team is divided into two parallel lines, about fifteen yards apart. One line is the ball carriers, another the defenders. I was in the 'ball carrier' line. When I'd get to the front of the line, the coach would blow his whistle and I would run toward a cone that was positioned about twenty yards out, in between the two lines, meaning I would be running at an angle, and the defender would be trying to hit me as hard as he could from his angle. Thus the name "angle drill."

It sounds much less sadistic than it really is. It served the dual purpose of teaching us to tackle while giving adults an excuse to watch kids try and hurt each other.

When you're in line, you start counting. With half fear, half anticipation, you count to see how many people are in front of you, and then you count that same number in the opposing line to see who you will be going up against. I was seventh in line. So I began counting the other line.

One, Two, Three, Four, Five, Six... Oh God...

Now, I will admit, my memory is probably taking extreme liberties here, but when I got to number seven, there stood a kid named Hendricks, who looked like a miniature Eric Dickerson. Jerry curl, goggles, headband, and all. In my exaggerated memory, he was foaming at the mouth like he had rabies, licking his lips at the prospect of going against the white boy who showed up late and got tired running from one coach to another.

In hindsight I was just extremely unlucky, because Hendricks was indeed the hardest hitter on our team. And at that moment, he was going to deliver the first hit I'd ever received in football.

I got to the front and I was absolutely terrified. To my core. Shaking scared. I had no idea what I was doing or what I was about to do or what I was supposed to do.

Please, let me just go back into the unlit parking lot where it's safe. It's cool. They know my dad.

I didn't know how to hold a football or how to take a hit or how to deliver a hit. Nothing. I had never even watched football on TV.

My dad stood nearby watching, sucking on a cigarette, smoke floating over the line of football players.

Like I said: Football's Golden Age.

Without warning, Coach Layne blew his whistle, which was my cue to start running toward the cone. I ran like my life depended on it, which, as far as I was concerned, it did. For a split second, I thought *maybe if I run as fast as I can, I'll just outrun him.*

Bad decision.

What little speed I had just lent toward a greater collision. A one-sided collision. A tragic, horrific collision.

It sounded like a car crash. I just crumpled to the ground with Hendricks's assistance. To make matters worse, when he slammed me to the ground I was holding the football over my stomach, meaning I landed on top of it with such force that the air in my lungs decided to momentarily vacate my body.

I saw white from the impact and I couldn't breathe.

Now as an adult, you know if you get the wind knocked out of you that it's coming back eventually. But as a seven-year-old, you don't quite have that life experience to fall back on. So I panicked.

I can't breathe. I Can't Breathe! I CAN'T BREATHE! I CAN'T FUCKING BREATHE.

I was trying to cry, but crying requires air, so I just gasped. And gasped. And weezed. And gasped some more. I held my mouth open, hoping oxygen might accidentally drift its way in, which it did not.

While tears streamed down my cheeks and oxygen was nowhere to be found, my dad strolled up, casual as ever, Marlboro Red between his lips, Hawaiian shirt half unbuttoned, walking along as if he was surveying a used car on a car lot, more intrigued than concerned.

"Jas, just relax," he said, as if that were possible in that moment. "You just got the wind knocked out of you."

Fuck you, Dad.

I could hear the group in the parking lot yelling at me.

"Get up, Jas, don't let him see you hurt," one hollered, making me feel slightly encouraged until I heard another yell, "DAMN, HE GOT LIT THE FUCK UP!"

As the air slowly returned to my body, I laid there, looking up at the evening sky, my peripheral blinded by the stadium lights, thinking only one thing:

I will never go to the grocery store with my dad again.

Thankfully, that day's practice got called early because there was a drive-by shooting at the school.

"Oh," I remember thinking. *"Thank God for drive-by shootings. Whatever that means."*

I didn't really know what a "drive-by shooting" was. I knew they were usually preceded by someone letting off what I assumed were firecrackers, sometimes followed by grown women screaming and crying. Often times there'd be screeching tires. Lots of yelling. Cussing. The coaches would look at each other like soldiers who were fighting a war they knew they were losing. No matter what was happening at practice, as soon as the firecrackers went off, they gathered us together, told us how important school was and then tell us to go home quickly.

I'd go home tired, bruised, hot, sweaty, and hope to God that we'd get lucky and have a drive-by shooting again tomorrow.

———

"So football became an escape from some pretty traumatic experiences for you from the outset?"

"Yeah," I told him, "I guess so. I never really thought about it like that."

"I heard you were pretty good," he said, referring to the player I eventually became.

"Yeah, I was OK."

"You got recruited?" he asked.

"Yeah, at the beginning of my sophomore year the schools started showing up, pulling me out of class--"

"The same year your uncle died."

I immediately realized he was less interested in my skills on the football field, and more interested in the timing.

"So your uncle dies, and you dive into the one thing in which you'd always been able to find an escape: football."

Silence.

He gave me a look that begged 'you see where I'm going with this?'

"Yeah, I guess I did," I said, thinking out loud. "I mean, it worked pretty well. That's not unhealthy is it?"

"You tell me," he countered. "How healthy was it?"

"It wasn't a problem," I explained, "until it was taken from me."

CHAPTER 3.

ONE HIT

I wonder if Mark is looking down at me. Or worse, looking up.

"Huddle up!" barked out Kyle, our quarterback.

Does dying of a heroin overdose mean you go to hell? I mean, if that was a sin, and that was the last thing he ever did, is he in hell?

"Jason! Huddle up!" he yelled, trying to snap me back into reality as I wandered in the direction of the huddle.

Maybe he's in heaven, looking down. Does he feel guilty? Can you feel guilt in heaven? Is he watching my game right now? Can he see me?

"Alright, green right flip 34 power pass Y-screen," says Kyle, he and I making eye contact. The ball is coming to me.

Is there a heaven? Or a hell? Or a God?

"On one."

If there's a God, why did he let this happen?

"Ready…"

CLAP

The huddle sets about eight yards behind the line of scrimmage, allowing a quick survey of the defense as we jogged forward and got set. I saw they were playing a cover-3 defense with the corners cheating up to stop the run. "Green right" normally meant that I, as the strong-side tight end, would line up to the right, but the "flip" meant exactly what it sounds like—that I'd be on the left.

At the varsity level, the defense would have picked up on this immediately. The strong-side tight end lining up weak side should be a dead giveaway, but being that this was a junior varsity game and their coaches probably had better shit to do on a Saturday than watch game film, they didn't suspect a thing.

In football, like poker, you play the eyes. That linebacker who has been keying an offensive lineman all game is suddenly looking in the backfield? He's coming on a blitz. A corner who doesn't make eye contact with me when I'm his key? I'm running right by him. Are they tired? Scared? Confused? Concussed?

It's all in the eyes.

"DOWN... BLACK 13, BLACK 13," hollered Kyle.

This was just a decoy. "Black" meant we were running the play we called in the huddle.

Looking up, I watched the corner creep forward, ever so slightly. He was anticipating a run to the opposite side. His tells were minute—putting just a bit more weight on his left foot, placing his right foot just a bit further behind his right.

Come on, come on. That's it...you're gonna help backside protection. Creep forward, creep forward...that's it...come on...

This corner and I had a brief history.

A quarter earlier, he got in my face after a cheap shot. I didn't see him coming and he took me out from the side. It was a good hit that I probably would have let go if he would have just shut the fuck up.

But he didn't do that.

"You like that?" he screamed, all amped up, jumping around. "That hurts, huh?" as I picked myself up off the ground.

Hurts? You want to talk about hurt motherfucker? I'm three weeks removed from giving mouth-to-mouth to my dying uncle, tasting him die. Every time I put my mouthpiece in I think about it.

That's what hurt feels like.

I wanted him to hurt. I wanted him to hurt like I hurt. I wanted someone to share this feeling with, to soak with me in whatever the fuck it was that I was feeling.

"HUT!"

The ball was snapped and I took an inside step, pass-blocking the defensive end who thought we were throwing the ball strong side. I've played defensive end, and when you see a right-handed quarterback set up to throw, your eyes get big. Your mouth waters. He'll never see you coming.

Which was exactly what we wanted him to think.

With the play and all of its momentum going right, I stepped back and the QB tossed the ball in my direction. The whole defense took an "oh shit" step, completely out of position, leaving only my friend, the corner, to beat.

It would've been an easy touchdown. The corner was out of position and all I needed to do was hit the sideline. He'd never catch me. I'd run right by him.

But I didn't want to run by him. I wanted to hurt him.

I angled to the inside, running directly toward him. A touchdown wouldn't provide the relief I needed. I needed someone to share this pain with, and by mouthing off, this kid became an unwitting accomplice in my search for clarity and comprehension of the incomprehensible.

He put his head down, a no-no. You learn early on

in football that if you don't keep your head up, you get hurt. This kid decided he'd rather turn his body into an unguided missile, hoping someone from our team just happened across his path. I dropped my shoulder, trying to concentrate all of my speed and strength and pain and hurt into one point of contact — one collision.

CRACK.

I heard that sound and knew right away it was bad. It sounded like the cracking of a shoulder pad, but I knew it wasn't my shoulder, and he led with his head, so it wasn't his.

I got up off the ground and looked down. He just lay there. No motion. No movement. He was on his back, looking up at the sky, scared to death. A mind trapped in a body that wouldn't respond. His eyes darted between the sky and me, sky and me, sky and me.

It was his neck. That sound I heard... it was his neck.

I wanted to motion to the sideline for a doctor, but I couldn't move. I was frozen, looking down at him. And he, looking up at me.

The referee approached and immediately knew something was wrong. This kid, eyes wide, mouth closed, body still, wasn't getting up. The blur of referees and coaches and paramedics and players — is just that. A blur.

I didn't snap out of it until I saw his parents approach. Their son lay on the field, facemask cut off, strapped down to a stretcher to keep any movement from further destroying his mangled spine. An ambulance drove out to the 40-yard line where the medics lifted him inside, while Mom looked down and told him it would be okay. Dad stood off to the side of the ambulance, not saying a word, while a team doctor explained that a broken neck didn't necessarily mean permanent paralysis.

But I was just watching him. *He had weight on his left leg, right foot back. He was moving. I was trying to hurt him...*

The fans and players clapped as the ambulance drove off the field, a strange gesture when you think about it. You know the kid can't hear you, and you know the paramedics are busy in their attempt of stabilization, but you clap anyway. Truth is, you're not really clapping for the kid or the doctors or the driver. You're clapping for yourself, hoping that somehow, some way, you can wrap your mind around what you just saw happen — a 14-year-old kid break his neck while playing a game — and process it to the point of forgetting it and moving on. You clap at the end of a play, or a movie, or a concert. It's finality, your way of moving on to whatever comes next.

And just like that, the referee blew the whistle to continue play.

You know that little place inside where things are stuffed deep down, safe from conscious thought, contemplation, and clear recollection? Well, it has a basement.

The good news: The door to that basement locks up nice and tight, taking years to pry open.

The bad news: The door to that basement locks up nice and tight, taking years to pry open.

Our team defeated Folsom High School that day, but I lost. Coming on the heels of Mark's overdose, this kid's broken neck pushed me to a point of feeling so much guilt that my brain's only coping mechanism was to eliminate "guilt" completely.

The shame I felt was immense, stronger than anything I'd ever felt in my 14 years of life. The self-hatred was unhealthy, consuming my every thought.

I learned to live like that for the next 3 years. I began

carrying around a razor blade in my wallet, tucked into a place that only I knew existed, just in case.

In case of what? I didn't know. But I felt better knowing that it was there.

I'd look in the mirror and think, *what would have happened if you'd called 911 the morning Mark died? He'd be here, wouldn't he?* Stomachache, look away.

I'd put my shoes on and think, *it feels good to be able to move your legs, doesn't it? I wonder who's dressing that paraplegic this morning?* Stomachache, think of something else.

I'd see an ambulance driving and have this twisted fantasy of Mark and the kid with the broken neck lying down, side-by-side. *I bet they're talking mad shit about you right now.* Stomachache, close my eyes and just breathe.

It was fucked up.

Three. Long. Years.

Almost three years to the day of breaking a kid's neck, I was sitting in a small Toyota Celica at a red light. I didn't even see the car approaching in my rearview; it happened so fast.

CRACK.

I felt the pain shoot down my left leg, realizing immediately that something was wrong. I automatically assumed this was karma. This is how the universe works. That long, moral arc, so vast, but always fair.

But I could still move. I was alive. I wasn't paralyzed. Those voices, that pain, the shame and self-hatred still active, the ability to feel guilt still amputated. Nothing was different.

At the hospital they told me they'd need to put a titanium cage in my spine to fuse a disc.

"Jason," the doctor told me, "we're going to give you a shot of Demerol, something for the pain."

"Demerol?" I asked, watching him shoot the clear liquid directly into the vein on top of my left hand. "What's Demer... oh... oh wow... oh fu... that feels goo..." Closing my eyes with my head falling forward, I felt saturated in warmth and comfort, melting into my hospital bed while my eyes paid their respects by going half-mast.

That first hit. There's nothing like it in the natural world. I was in love. This feeling? I didn't want it to stop. I wanted to feel this way forever.

And ever.

The shame. The self-hatred. The guilt. It disappeared.

My uncle? Didn't care. Not my problem.

That kid who broke his neck? Should've kept his head up when he tackled me. Wish him the best, XOXO...

Gone. Poof, just like that. Nothing mattered. My insecurities, my fears, all gone.

People always wonder why drug addicts do drugs, even after our lives are destroyed by the inability to stop. You don't understand why we do drugs?

We don't understand why you don't.

We do it for this. This feeling, right here. Nothing matters. Nothing hurts.

From that day forward, I'd chase that feeling. From zero to forever with one shot to the vein.

I was 17 years old.

"Jason," asked the doctor, "is that enough or do you need a little bit more?"

I just looked at him, not a care in the world, all smiles, warm and cozy in my own skin for the first time in a long time.

"More, please."

"Oh shit, that first taste!" said my sponsor, excited and laughing. *"We always remember that first one."*

Though I didn't realize it at the time, this was precisely why talking to this guy was about to save my life. I'd been to rehabs. Plural. And while well-intentioned, they didn't work because none of those counselors truly understood what it meant to be a drug addict. I'm sure they studied hard for their online courses, reading about the science of addiction, the dopamine, serotonin, neurotransmitters, reward-centers of the brain, frontal lobe, etc. etc. etc., but none of them knew what it felt like to wake up and NEED the drug. None of them had ever been to that place where you're willing to take everything you love, everything you cherish in life, everything that's important to you, and move it to the side in an attempt to score just one more time. You know that feeling of having your head held under water, the last of your oxygen depleted, where every fiber of your being screams at you to get to the surface for more air? That's the feeling of needing more drugs, the trepidation of normalcy creeping in. No counselor who never knew that feeling could ever help me.

A fellow drug addict though? He knew that feeling because he lived through it, and for me, that was the most important thing. My sponsor had a GED from Folsom Prison and knew more about me than any non-addict with a PhD ever could.

It's nothing against non-addict counselors. They're doing the best they can with the knowledge they have. But an addict recognizes another addict the same way a war veteran recognizes another veteran. You don't even have to say anything – there's a silent understanding. Hell leaves a scar recognizable only to other addicts.

"Yeah, man, that first taste," I repeated, almost longingly, my voice trailing off. Staring off into the distance, I watched a horse graze while the mere discussion of that first hit made my chest feel warm.

"How long did it take?" he asked, snapping me back to the present.

"How long did what take?"

"How long did it take," he continued, "to go from guy-using-medication-for-his-back to guy-completely-destroying-his-life-while-chasing-a-high?"

The question made me smile and the answer made me laugh.

"About a day," I said, both of us cracking up, not because it was funny, but because it was absurd.

I could just shake my head. "It took a day."

CHAPTER 4.

MACBETH-UAL HEALING

I remember where I was standing, what I was wearing, what the weather was like that day. Sierra College campus next to the library there's a bench, next to wooden pillars where people post multi-colored flyers about rooms for rent, cars for sale, tutoring services. Blue jeans and a black hoodie, gray beanie. Foggy and overcast, chilly with a chance of rain.

I had a bottle of Norco 10-325, a powerful semi-synthetic opioid derived from codeine, which I'd been taking for about a week. I was prescribed 1-2 tablets every 6 hours, which, when taken as prescribed, gave me a little buzz, but nothing like that shot of Demerol in the hospital.

I had a bottle of Soma, a skeletal muscle relaxant. I was prescribed 1 tablet every 6 hours, which, when taken as prescribed, just made me fall asleep.

I had me, a broken kid who just had the only thing he'd ever been good at taken away. I could no longer play the game that had been my refuge since I was seven-years-old. I needed a new numbing agent at the exact time one was offered to me.

Oxygen, by itself, is our life-force as human beings. It is the third most abundant element in our universe. Without oxygen, there would be no life.

Fire, by itself, can be controlled, allowing human beings to evolve out of the Stone Age as we gained the ability to cook food, create heat, and manufacture light.

Gasoline, by itself, is harmless. An air-tight barrel of gasoline poses no threat or danger on its own.

But mix the three together just right...

I'd never even smoked weed before, and had gotten drunk three times in high school, at most. I was what I believe history will come to know as a millennial drug addict, an addict who didn't seek out the drugs, didn't seek out the high. Rather, the drugs and the high found me, and it was love at first sight.

I had half an hour to kill before my English class, and I began wondering what would happen if I took the medications together. Not only that, but what if instead of taking the medication as prescribed on the bottle, I just took my entire day's Norco and Soma at one time? What would happen? I was allowed 8 Norco and 4 soma per-day, per the directions on the bottle. But fuck the directions on the bottle. What did I have to lose?

In hindsight, the answer to this question is about 16 years of life. At the time, my attitude was simply, "fuck it."

I was after that high I felt in the hospital, the immense relief I felt as the Demerol traced its way through my veins, to my chest, and pumped out from there. Following the directions on the bottle wasn't doing the trick, so I took matters into my own hands, imposing the "self" in "self-medicating."

Grabbing the red Gatorade from my backpack, I washed down all 12 pills, 2 at a time, before beginning my 15 minute walk to the classroom. We were having a debate in class on the death penalty, and my plan was to keep quiet and fantasize about Briana, the girl who sat next to me in class and with whom I had never even spoken because she was way too good looking for someone like me.

At the exact moment I walked into class, I got hit in the chest by something warm and seductive. I steadied myself against the doorway with my mouth open and eyes opened wide, hunched over, trying to understand what was happening to me. It was like a medical emergency but the opposite, a reverse heart attack. Instead of panic there was pleasure. Instead of hyperventilation, my breathing slowed. It felt like I had warm water flowing through my veins, my joints soaking in narcotic indulgence.

Oh my God, I thought. *That... feels...fucking... incre...di...ble...*

"Jason, are you ok?" asked Franklin, one of those cool professors who went by his first name.

I just looked at him and smiled.

"Fuckin-Aye, Franklin," I said to the astonishment of my classmates. They looked to the professor, awaiting his response. He started cracking up laughing, setting the tone for class that day as he asked me to have a seat.

From my seat I exuded confidence. Jumping in and out of the death penalty debate with witty remarks and factual backing, I was suddenly smart. "Holy shit," I said under my breath. "These drugs also make me intelligent." I had always hated school with a passion. I found homework tedious and lectures redundant. But high, I could function. I actually enjoyed this shit.

As the death penalty debate raged on in class, I leaned over to Briana, the girl who was out of my league.

"Hey," I said twice, she either not hearing me or ignoring me the first time. "Hey. I'm Jason, and I just wanted to say that you look really pretty today."

She started blushing and smiled, mouthing the words "thank you."

Without drugs I was a shy, teenage boy who never would have talked to this girl. High, I had game.

"Hey," I said, glancing toward the professor to make sure he wasn't taking notice of my first-ever seduction of a female. "How come we've never hung out?"

She shrugged her shoulders.

The drugs were really doing their thing by now. "I think we should do something about that," I told her, still glancing in the direction of the professor from time to time.

Looking in my direction, she mouthed the words, "I have a boyfriend."

Without missing a beat, I mouthed the words, "I don't care."

She looked at me and squinted with a mischievous smile.

"When?" she asked.

"Right now," I said, before even thinking about it.

Briana smiled and shook her head no. "Tonight," she said, and wrote down her number on a piece of paper and handed it to me. Next to the number she scribbled "Macbeth?" I had no idea what this meant.

Macbeth? Who's Macbeth? Why do I know that name?

"Ok," said Franklin, before I had a chance to decipher Briana's code, "thank you guys, great work today. I'll see you Monday." Standing up to leave the room, he called me over. "Jason," he said, "can I talk to you for a minute?"

Fuck. I was certain I was busted. I was so high that

I couldn't feel my face, my insides microwaved to a comfortable temperature and my eyelids beginning to sag ever-so-slightly.

"Hey, Jason," began Franklin, "I just wanted to say great work today. I really enjoyed having you in the debate. Really nice work."

Is he being sarcastic?

"How'd it go with Briana?" he asked once she left the room.

"What? Briana? Who?"

"Come on, I'm not an idiot," he said, talking to me like a person rather than a student, something I'd never experienced with a teacher before. "Are you guys coming tonight?"

"Are we coming where?"

"To the play in midtown," Franklin said. "*Macbeth.*"

"*Macbeth?*"

"The extra credit I gave out. You guys are welcome to come," he said, as I began to thoroughly support getting high as an academic plan. "Anyway, I just wanted to say great work in the discussion today. I've never seen this side of you."

Me neither.

"Thanks, man. I'll see if I can make it tonight," I told him.

Finishing my last class for the week, I walked to my car and felt alive. I felt good. I felt comfortable, confident. I was a new person, thanks to Dr. Rhiner and his powers of prescribing. This feeling…warm, blissful euphoria, THIS feeling… 16 years later when I woke up in bloody bathwater to the pain of living, wanting nothing more than to go back to the way things were in the beginning, when drugs were fun and I was indestructible, this was the feeling I longed for, that I sought. I wanted nothing more than to go back to the beginning, to THIS.

But it doesn't work that way.

That road don't go where it used to. There comes a threshold in addiction, a point of no return, when the drugs go from being a luxury to a necessity, from fun to misery. Once you cross that threshold, it's game over. You're fucked and there's no going back. That road took me to depths I could never have possibly imagined I'd see on that first day, sitting there flirting with Briana. There was no way of knowing it at the time, but my journey to hell and back had begun.

But in the meantime––back to Briana.

Briana was sexy. Slightly bigger than skinny but not quite thick, she had a body that didn't need to be flaunted with low-cut tops and miniskirts. She dressed well, covering up but letting you know there was something underneath, wavy blonde hair and a cute face. I've always been a sucker for cute faces, and Briana didn't disappoint. She looked a few years older than me, placing her in what I guessed was her early 20s.

Still in communication's Golden Age, pre-text messaging, I called Briana later that evening, just as my high began wearing off. We chatted briefly about school, before she asked if I wanted to pick her up that night to go see *Macbeth*.

"Sure, I can do that," I told her.

"Ok, good. But I have to be home early in the morning," she explained. "I'm going to visit my dad in jail."

"Wai – what? Morning? Jail? Huh? You want me to take you home in the morning?"

"Yeah," she said in rapid-speak. "But it's got to be early. I'm visiting my dad. Shit, I have another call. See you at 7."

And just like that she hung up the phone.

My high completely gone by now, I began to panic. Briana wanted the me who was in class, the me high on Norco and Soma, the me with a confidence that I could not generate without chemicals. I was like a narcotic Teen Wolf.

Oh yeah, and I was a virgin.

Yep, 17 years old and still a virgin. For whatever reason, I was holding out for someone special. It didn't come from some religious or moral standing. I just wanted my first time to be something unique, with someone important, and that opportunity had yet to present itself. Sure, Briana was cute, and seemed like a nice girl, but she wasn't exactly the girl I felt comfortable calling my first.

Fuck, fuck, fuck. I don't want to have sex with this girl. She's got a dad in jail, who will probably get out and want to find the guy who just had sex with his daughter. I don't even know why he's in jail – probably for whipping the ass of the last guy she spent the night with. Dammit, why did I already take all of my pills for today?

I began devising a plan.

Ok Jason, calm down. Deep breaths. It's Friday. Just take Saturday's pills tonight, and just don't take any tomorrow. Yeah, that's the plan. Take tomorrow's today, and by Sunday you'll be back on track. Shit, you're a genius!

This is some straight drug addict reasoning and rationale, derived from wherever addiction and dependence resides in the brain, and it happened without me even trying. It just happened. I didn't know it at the time, but my journey had begun. Before the addict manipulates and lies to others, he or she first manipulates and lies to themselves.

I learned to compartmentalize in a very schizophrenic

sense, a skill I'd use throughout my years of addiction. There was the "now me," which was the center of the universe, the only thing that really mattered, the most important person in the room. And then there was "tomorrow me," who would have much more will power, much more strength, and make much better decisions than "now me." To be honest, I really didn't give much of a shit about "tomorrow me." "Tomorrow me" would be able to go without pills for a day. "Tomorrow me" would be able to get through the day because he had will power, a strength that "now me" didn't possess. "Tomorrow me" was of the utmost character, with integrity to spare. He could handle it.

Inevitably, tomorrow would come, creating a third character in this schizophrenic dance: "Yesterday me." Fuck, I hated "yesterday me." He was an inconsiderate asshole, leaving "now me" without any drugs, nothing to make myself feel different. I hated "yesterday me" with a passion. I've woken up in jails, strange houses, gutters, hospitals, all thanks to whatever "yesterday me" did, leaving "now me" to deal with the fucking wreckage. Every morning I'd wake up with the same thought: Fuck you "yesterday me."

Like I said: Schizophrenic.

Pulling into Briana's driveway, I washed down Saturday's pills on a Friday night: 8 Norco and 4 Soma. Stepping out of my car, Briana walked out of her front door while her mom pulled the living room curtain back to have a look at me. Briana wore a long, black dress with heels, her hair pulled up, exposing a neck that doubled as an invitation. I nodded a "hello" to her mom, who continued to watch suspiciously as Briana walked up and gave me a hug before getting into the car.

The first 10 minutes were awkward. I had no idea what to say to this girl as I waited for my high to commence.

"Umm...so *Hamlet*, huh?" I said, timidly.

"You mean *Macbeth*?" she asked in a tone that prayed I was joking.

"Yeah, sorry... *Macbeth*... of course..."

Silence. Awkward, brutal, uncomfortable silence.

Finally, my toes finally began to tingle. The warmth traveled up through my legs, into my hips, straight to my stomach, over my chest, up my neck before finally hitting my head.

Woooooooosh.

"You look nice, by the way," I said, suddenly self-assured and confident.

"Thank you," she replied. "I thought you might like this dress."

"You thought right."

"So, like I said," Briana explained, "I have a boyfriend, so we can't..."

I cut her off. "Listen, I don't really care much about your personal life. What you got going with him is none of my business, just like what happens tonight is none of his."

She looked shocked by my bluntness, but in a satisfied sort of way.

"Sounds like a plan," she finally said, looking ahead.

Parking the car on J Street, we got out and Briana walked over to me, grabbed my hand, and put it around her waist. Looking up, she gave me a kiss that suggested the rest of the night was going to be full of lust and bad decisions.

The class met outside of the theater, and Franklin looked genuinely happy to see us.

"Hey," he yelled out as we walked. "You guys made it."

"Wouldn't miss it for the world," I told him.

We sat in the rear of the theater, Briana and me at the end of the row, next to the wall. As the play began, Briana put her hand on my knee. As witches made the decision to meet a guy named Macbeth, Briana made the decision to inch her hand up my leg. Looking over, I could see the girl next to Briana take notice. From time to time she'd glance over at Briana's hand, which wasn't even attempting discretion. As that Macbeth guy killed somebody named Duncan, Briana slid her hand down my pants and gave me a kiss on the neck. I had no idea if the rest of the class took notice or not, because at that moment my thoughts were occupied by other things.

As Act II got underway, Briana asked if I'd come with her to get some water. Inching our way down the aisle, Franklin giving me a knowing glance, Briana walked to the back of the theater. The walls of the theater had thick curtains all the way around. Looking back at me Briana smiled, and slid behind one of the curtains that were about 10 feet from where our class was sitting. I followed. In the dark I could feel her unbutton my pants and put her back up against the wall. As she kissed me, I slid my hand up her leg to her inner-thigh, discovering she wasn't wearing panties. Reaching down, she grabbed me and put me inside of her.

Just like that.

No condom. No consideration of consequences. No nothing. It was all out the window. The deterioration and complete abandonment of any and all morals, ethics, whatever. In one day, I went from shy virgin who'd never touched drugs to fucking the hot girl in class behind a curtain while the class watched a play.

In one day. Talk about positive reinforcement.

"Tomorrow me" could worry about things like pregnancy, STDs, the fact that I just lost my virginity – something I was trying to hold onto until the right time – to a girl whose last name I didn't know. "Tomorrow me" could wake up and think *what in the fuck did I just do*. After all, he was the responsible one. "Now me" was busy with the girl I was too shy to talk to without drugs.

I had no idea what I was doing. Looking back on it I probably owe her an apology, because I'm fairly certain my sloppy attempt at sex failed miserably. I was clueless. Thankfully, Briana knew precisely what she was doing. While someone named Lady Macbeth spoke, I held my hand over Briana's mouth so that she wouldn't make any noise. She looked me in the eyes, her left leg wrapped around me, dress pulled up to her waist, sliding her way up and down the theater wall.

As Lady Macbeth cried out, "That which hath made them drunk hath made me bold, what hath quenched them hath given me fire," Briana spoke in less eloquent phrasings. "We need to hurry," she whispered. "I want you to cum inside me."

Holy shit, I can't believe this is happening.

"I'll try."

"Cum inside me," she demanded, louder this time. "I want to feel it."

I closed my eyes and had to fantasize about having sex behind a theater curtain with the girl I was having sex with behind a theater curtain. The reality was too vivid, so I went to my imagination.

It worked.

Melting into my Norco and Soma high, I lost my virginity to a girl from my English class, 10 feet away from my fellow students who watched as Macbeth was swallowed whole by his own ambition.

She pulled me out of her as if she'd escaped the "just got fucked behind the curtain of a theater" hold before, slid her dress back down, and side-stepped out from behind the curtain. I balanced myself against the wall, trying to grasp the reality of what just happened.

We watched the rest of the play, I took Briana home, kissed her good night, and drove home, high and happy. My first day as a drug addict wrapped up in a neat little bow.

The following morning I woke up groggy. I had a full recollection of the night before, and the thought of it gave me a stomach ache. *What in the fuck was I thinking? What if she's pregnant? What if I caught something? Fuck you "yesterday me."*

This was my first encounter with "yesterday me," our first soirée in the world of pharmaceutical-grade narcotics. He not only left me with a stomach ache for having lost my virginity to what was for all intents and purposes a total stranger, without protection, behind a fucking theater curtain, but he left me with no drugs for the day.

Asshole.

Doing the only logical thing (taking no pills for the day was NOT logical) I dipped into Sunday's stash until my stomach ache of anxiety and regret went away completely. That night, my friends called and wanted to go out. For the occasion, I dipped into Monday's pills.

By the time the weekend was over, I was already taking my pills for Friday on Monday.

"Sounds about right," said my sponsor. "The first time I ever got drunk was on a Friday night. I went to class drunk every day after that."

"Did you just drink?" I asked him.

"Nope, but I never got into too much trouble with alcohol," he said. "But once coke and meth entered the picture, the cops weren't far behind."

We both laughed because we'd both been there.

"What did that look like?" I asked.

"They sent me to a boys' camp in 11th grade," he said. "There, I learned how to do drugs for real. I learned how to cook it, cut it, all of it. It was like a university for a drug addict. I connected with the Mexicans who knew the people bringing it up, and that's when I really got fucked up. That's when I really got into the game."

"It's funny, because we really weren't that different, you and I," I told him. "The only difference was my dealers wore white lab coats."

"What do you mean?" he asked.

"I mean, after my back surgery, I could get anything I wanted just by lifting my shirt and showing my scars," I explained. "I was at the right place at the right time. Late 90s – early 2000s, they were giving that shit out like candy."

"So do you blame the doctors?" he asked.

"Yes," I told him.

"So it was their fault?" he kept pushing.

"Yeah, it was," I said.

"So innocent little Jason never manipulated the doctors, never lied to them, never pretended he wasn't a drug addict just so he could score stronger drugs?"

"Well, I mean...I...it's like...I couldn't..." was all I could mutter.

"I'm sure you were always honest with the doctors and discussed your situation with the pharmacists that you blame," he said, sarcastically but sincere.

I looked down, silently.

He wasn't finished. "Poor Jason, the victim, just pranced into the doctor's office, innocent as could be, and had drugs pushed on him, and took them because he had no other choice?"

I kept looking down.

"At some point, you have to take accountability for your actions and your choices. As long as you blame the doctors, it's their fault, and as long as it's their fault, you can't do shit with your life. You can't do shit because they have complete power and control over your moving on. Don't you see? It's always someone else's fault, and you need to take that bullshit somewhere else, because I don't want to hear it. Now, I'll be the first to say that something needs to change with the way doctors prescribe that shit. But neither of us has control over that. What we do have control over is our lives and our decisions, and all of this you're telling me about – you need to own that shit. To blame anyone other than yourself, in your situation, is a fucking death sentence," he said, letting those last three words hang in the air for a bit before continuing.

"Or maybe you'll get lucky and die, who knows?" he said. " Dying would be much better than living your life, blaming others, the perpetual victim of everyone around him, constantly numbing the guilt and shame you feel because deep down, even you know it's bullshit."

I wanted to cry but fought the feeling. I knew what he was

saying was true, and I had no response to it. Truth hadn't been a part of my life for so long that its presence stung, meaning silence was the only way I knew to respond.

I'm sure that a counselor at one of my rehabs had probably told me this same thing, but it was different coming from my sponsor, because he'd been where I was. He knew what I was going through. Usually, had another man said the things he was saying to me, it would've been on. There would've been a fight. But in this moment, at this time, I was letting what he told me sink in and permeate my thick skull. From him, it meant something.

I wanted to tell him to fuck off, that he was wrong, that he didn't have a clue what I was going through. I wanted to tell him that he didn't know me, that it wasn't my fault, that I was a victim of a fucked up system. I wanted to get up and walk back to my car, safe and sound in my self-loathing and denial. But instead I remained seated, and when I opened my mouth, all I could manage was a feeble, "you're right."

Now those two words hung in the air, replacing the old ones just in time.

"Now," he said, "tell me about your switch from pills to the Fentanyl patches, and when you do, don't make yourself the victim. Take accountability."

CHAPTER 5.

NEVER TRUST A RUSSIAN PROSTITUTE

Hiding outside of my own apartment, ducked down in the freezing Prague rain, I watched through a back window as the man wearing a black beanie went through my things and took anything that was of value. It was wet, mud caked up to my knees in the shivering cold. It seemed like a dream as I watched him take my DVDs, CDs, television, DVD player, laptop. The Russian Mafia didn't fuck around, but Sara had warned me of this. I just didn't listen.

A year prior to hiding from the Russian Mafia in the Czech Republic, I graduated from UC Davis with a degree in history. Somehow. The Norco and Soma were doing a number on me. I'd wrecked 4 cars, and each time the highway patrol on the scene gave me a breathalyzer to see if I'd been drinking. I blew zeroes, so they let me go. They weren't hip to the pill game just yet.

Luckily I never hurt anyone. Or maybe I did. Maybe I sent someone else on their own journey through the prescription drug world thanks to an accident that my addiction caused. I'll never know.

I graduated college on what I call the 10-20 plan. I'd get

a prescription for the pills, and a 30 day supply would last me 10 days. I'd take the pills and nod out in class, pass out at red lights, get fucked up beyond recognition, until the pills were gone. At that time, kicking after I ran out of the pills didn't seem that bad. I'd get sick for a day or two, but could tough it out. I'd go 20 days clean, during which I absorbed the material necessary to graduate, before getting my refill and doing it all over again.

I did this for 4 years. Over and over and over and over again.

By the time I graduated college, my friends had had enough of my shit, which was funny because I rarely saw them sober. But their drug of choice was alcohol, and that was more acceptable. I can't say I really blame them. I wouldn't have wanted to be around me. It must have looked crazy. I'd show up to their house sober, normal, coherent. I'd ask to use their bathroom, and immediately go through their medicine cabinet to see if there was anything there I could use. Usually there wasn't, leaving me with the drugs I had on me. After taking the Norco-Soma combination, I would emerge from the bathroom normal as could be. I'd grab a beer and just hold it. I hated the taste of alcohol, even beer, but I figured that if I was holding a beer, that would explain the behavior that was to come.

Well before anyone got drunk, the pills would hit me. Pretending the effects were from the beer I was holding was laughable, in a really tragic sense. I'd be sitting there with a group of friends while they talked about whatever was going on in their lives or some memory we had from high school, and in my brain there was a-whole-nother scenario playing out that had absolutely nothing to do with anything they were talking about. I mean, totally different scenario, on a completely different plane of existence. Nothing to do with anything in the real world and certainly nothing to do with the conversation "we" were having.

It was all good as long as the scenario remained in my head. But it never did. Every time, it would decide at some inappropriate time to jump into the real world, the real conversation, exposing the drug addict I'd become and the crazy shit that was playing out in my mind via the mindless babble produced by my lips. My friends just looked on and shook their heads while I pretended the beer I hadn't sipped once all night was really fucking me up.

They'd be having a conversation about a new job one of them had, as a mail-runner for an auto insurance company. Out of nowhere, I'd blurt out, "It's underneath the dashboard, but they'll never find it."

Silence. Silence. Silence.

They'd look at me, with a look begging "what the fuck?" like it's never been begged before. I just stood there, realizing what I just said, when I said it, and who I said it to, while also wondering what the fuck was underneath the dashboard.

It was ugly.

The week after receiving my diploma I met with my doctor, Dr. Mavens, my "pain management" doctor. He'd been supplying my drug habit for a few years, ever since Dr. Rhiner retired. I knew that I was entering the "real world" now, where I would need to find a job and be a productive member of society. At the urging of my family, I came clean to him about my pill habit.

"Look, man, I'm abusing the shit out of the pills you're

prescribing me," I told him, high, which was ironically appropriate.

"Really?" he asked.

"Yes."

"That's funny, because normally I can tell when my patients are abusing the meds I prescribe. Are you sure?"

Dude, I'm fucking high RIGHT NOW.

"Yeah, I'm sure. Your prescriptions are only lasting me 10 days, on a good month."

"I see…" as his voice trailed off.

I sat looking up at him from the examination table, expecting him to give me a lecture but hopeful he'd give me something to make the kick a little easier. Kicking was getting harder and harder the longer I used.

"Maybe the meds we're prescribing aren't handling your pain," he said, thinking out loud. "I think that's why you're abusing the meds, and probably why I didn't see the signs. It's not enough."

I could tell that somehow, my abusing the meds hurt his pride.

"Not enough?" I asked him.

"Not enough. Look, there's a medication that's out that is doing wonders for some of my patients," he explained. "It's called Fentanyl and it comes in a patch. The nice thing is, you can't abuse it. You just put a patch on your skin, and change it every three days. Someone your size, you'll probably need to change it every two days," he said, the mad scientist diagnosing as he went. "I think you're a prime candidate for the Fentanyl patch."

"But I came here to try and get off of the meds," I told him, reaching the limits of the honesty I was willing to face.

"I think you should try these patches. They'll really help with your back," he said.

I was at a crossroads. I wanted to get off of the meds, to cut the chain that tied me to a doctor in perpetuity. But at the same time, more drugs sounded like a great idea.

"Umm… yeah, I'll give it a shot," I told him, against my own will. I wanted to stop, but I wasn't ready to stop.

"I'm going to prescribe you the Fentanyl, and the Norco, but the Norco is only for breakthrough pain," he said as he wrote my script. "Only take it when you really need it."

"Oh, ok… yeah, that works," I said, hating myself for saying it.

Looking back, this would have been an excellent time to tell my doctor to go fuck himself. This would have been the perfect time to ask him about any kickbacks he got from the various pharmaceutical companies who made these drugs. It would have been the perfect opportunity to inquire as to how much training he had on the long-term effects of opiates, or how much training he'd had on these drugs beyond what the pharmaceutical sales representatives told him. I should have asked him why he wanted to keep me on the drugs that I'd arrived intending to get off of.

But I didn't ask any of these things because deep down I wanted to stay on the drugs. The addict that I am wasn't ready to stop. He was my dealer, and really – can you blame the dealer for wanting to keep his customers? In the street drug game, I was what you'd call a "knock," named such because they are constantly knocking on the dealer's door, wanting more. Needing more.

I was Dr. Maven's knock and he wanted to keep me around. Truth is, I let this happen. I could have walked out that day with nothing, committed to getting clean and avoiding the next nine years of addiction and jail overdoses and interventions and detoxes and rehabs and lawyers and courtrooms.

But I decided to stay on the drugs. It was my decision. He was just my dealer, and you can't fault the dealer for dealing. It's what they do.

With my degree in-hand, I needed a change of scenery. I'd burned all of my bridges in California. Shit, I was burning bridges before I even got to them. My sophomore year of college I'd studied abroad in Florence, Italy, and while abroad I didn't use drugs. I was happy. I decided the problem wasn't me – it was my location. I went back to Florence and got my degree to teach English as a foreign language. From there, I traveled to Prague, ready to start fresh with my Fentanyl patches and Norco tucked safely inside my carry-on luggage.

I applied for and got a job at a small English school whose owner, Maksim, was a flamboyant homosexual. This guy was, like, in your face, rubbing up on my leg when he talked, gay. The drug addict in me knew I could manipulate the shit out of this situation. I'd let him flirt with me, go along with it, helping him decide which teacher to assign the next students to, which just so happened to be me.

I worked for Maksim for a month, when one of my students, Paxon, from Cologne, Germany, asked if I'd teach him in private lessons because he was sick of Maksim hitting on him. I siphoned off 3 other students from Maksim's school and taught private lessons for a few months out of my apartment. It paid the bills, but that was it. I had no disposable income.

I applied for a second job, with The English

Language Institute, and got it. Every morning I'd take the subway to various bank branches throughout Prague, teaching their executives Business English. I spent my days teaching corrupt bankers in a corrupt industry the difference between saying "I collapse the world economy" vs. "I collapsed the world economy" vs. "I will collapse the world economy."

Like I said, it paid the bills.

Dr. Mavens loaded me up with enough patches and Norco before I left to last me a few months. The patches didn't make me feel high, which was disappointing. The one thing they did, however, was keep me from getting sick once I ran through the Norco. By this point, a month's supply of Norco lasted me about eight days, meaning I easily had a 40 pill per-day habit. He prescribed me a quantity of 360, and that bottle would disappear quickly. When I ran out of the Norco, I'd put on two or three patches, and that would keep me from getting sick.

I discovered I was a fantastic teacher. I was high, but nobody knew – in fact, that was the only "me" they knew. I applied high, interviewed high, accepted the job high, and taught high. High became my normal, destroying any sense of true normalcy that I held onto in the beginning. That "me" who woke up after losing my virginity to Briana disappeared, the one who worried about pregnancy, STDs, bad decisions. The responsible one. I no longer knew that guy. That little voice, that spiritual connection to the rest of humanity that told me right from wrong, good from bad, beautiful from ugly – it was swallowed whole by the drugs. Gone. Poof, just like that. What remained was somebody so morally and spiritually bankrupt, that sex, drugs, more sex, and more drugs, simply became the norm.

My "normal" behavior became more and more extreme. The drugs gave me that confidence I had with Briana, and getting girls was easy. Too easy. I philandered and fucked my way across Italy and the Czech Republic, which brought me to Sara.

I don't know if Sara was her real name, but that doesn't matter. Sara was a prostitute from Russia who worked in one of the local "cabaret" clubs in Prague. Imagine a strip club with the most out-of-this-world attractive women your mind can conjure up. Now multiply the number of women you picture, outnumbering the many club patrons 3 to 1. Now, imagine there's an upstairs where you can have sex with these women.

That was the Czech version of a "cabaret."

I went to a cabaret out of curiosity once, but didn't pay for sex. I didn't have that kind of money. Plus, I was afraid of paying for sex, because I knew that with my personality, I'd start and never stop. So I went and just watched.

Sara worked in the club, and we seemed to hit it off, but you can never be sure in these types of establishments. They're paid to make you think they are falling in love with you, and they're good. But Sara seemed intrigued by my refusal to go upstairs, something she obviously wasn't used to. As I got up to go home, Sara asked me if I wanted to get breakfast after she got off at 9 o'clock in the morning. I obliged, and we formed a friendship.

I never had sex with Sara. It's funny that the one girl with whom I didn't have sex was the one who had sex for a living. She'd come over, drink, do lines of coke off my coffee table, and watch my *Saved by the Bell* DVDs.

As my platonic friendship with Sara grew, I started getting low on Fentanyl patches. I took a box to a doctor in Prague who seemed very surprised by a seemingly healthy, 23 year old male taking such a powerful drug, but I had a letter from Dr. Mavens that was translated into Czech, recommending to whatever doctor I found to prescribe the patches.

"This is very strong medicine," the doctor told me. "Eez like heroin."

"Heroin?" I asked. Dr. Mavens left that part out back in California.

"Yes, but more strong," the doctor said.

"Look, man, all I know is this is what my doctor gives me and I need it."

"I will give it," he told me, "but you must be very careful."

"Deal."

Taking my script to the pharmacy, the pharmacist looked down at the prescription, then up at me. Down at the prescription, up at me. Down, then up.

"You have cancer?" she asked me.

"Umm... I... don't... think... so," I replied.

"This is very strong medicine," she told me. "Eez like heroin."

"Yeah, that's what I hear," I said, getting impatient. "Look, can you fill it or not?"

"Yes," she told me as she walked to the back. Returning with three boxes of patches, the same brand I got in the US, she set them on the table.

"550 Euro, please," she said.

"550 Euro? What the fuck? That's how much they cost?"

"Yes."

"That's what I pay in rent," I told her, as if she gave a shit what my rent was. "I can't pay that!"

"I am sorry," pretended the pharmacist.

As I left the pharmacy, I knew I was in trouble. I was down to my last box of five patches, and while I hadn't kicked the Fentanyl before, something told me the withdrawal would be horrific. It was a strange medicine because just wearing a patch on my skin didn't get me high, but it gripped my soul much tighter than the pills ever did. Wearing it on my skin made it a part of me. I had an inner, subconscious clock that always let me know when it was time to change the patch. It had a much greater control over me than the pills ever did, and I feared that all of those kicks I'd avoided when I ran out of pills by using the patch were somehow absorbed into a single kick, just waiting for me to run out.

I was scared to death.

The next morning Sara came by for coffee, and I explained my predicament. I showed her my box of patches and told her there was no way I could afford to pay 550 Euro per month to get them in Prague.

Reading the box, Sara said, "Eez stronger than heroin."

"Ok, yeah, fuck, I get it, alright? It would've been nice to know that before I went on them," I said, annoyed and lying. I knew damn well I would've still taken the patches from my doctor on that first day had he told me they were stronger than heroin. But by proclaiming my ignorance to the Russian prostitute in my living room, I was making myself the poor, innocent victim.

I was good at that.

"You want heroin? I can get heroin," said Sara, matter-of-factly, like Walter in *The Big Lebowski* telling The Dude he could get a finger.

"No, Sara," I snapped, "I don't want heroin, thank you for offering. I just want the fucking patches."

"I can ask friend if he can get these," said Sara, writing down the information from the box. "That will help?"

With Sara sometimes it was best to not ask too many questions.

"Yes, that'd be wonderful. Thank you."

Two days later, Sara showed up at my apartment unannounced in the evening. She was wearing an overcoat over lingerie––an indication she'd been working that day. "Ok, Jason, my friend say he give you patches for 100 Euro."

She paused, hesitating with whatever was coming next. "But he say he want favor."

"Ok, great, thank you. I can do 100 Euro – wait, favor?"

"Yes, favor. He is Russian Mafia, Jason. He can get patch for you, but he want your apartment when you go to work," she explained.

"My apartment? For what?" I asked.

"I don't ask," she said, in a serious tone. "You don't ask too. It's for best."

"So he wants to use my apartment while I'm at work, and if I let him, he'll get me the patches for 100 Euro?"

"Yes," said Sara. "But Jason... Russians... don't fuck with Russians."

"Will he be gone when I get home?" I asked, slowly realizing the shitty situation I was in.

"He say he want your schedule and he is gone when you come home," said Sara, looking more worried than I would have liked.

The Russian Mafia had a heavy presence in Prague, so having them involved in day-to-day life wasn't all that abnormal. A few months earlier my apartment had been robbed, and at the suggestion of one of my students, I paid someone from the Russian Mafia to get my stuff back. Never mind the fact that it was more than likely the Russian Mafia who robbed my apartment to begin with. They served a purpose in Prague, and I needed their help.

"Ok, let's do it," I told Sara. "When can we get the patches?"

Reaching into her bag, Sara pulled out 3 boxes of Mylan Duragesic Fentanyl patches, the same brand I used at home and the same brand they had at the pharmacy in Prague where they asked for 550 Euro. I tried to pay Sara in Czech Crowns for the patches.

"They only want American dollars," she told me.

"Why?" I asked.

"Jason, don't ask questions."

I had to pull the money out of the ATM then take it to the bank to be converted in US Dollars, which was a pain in the ass and meant I was getting fucked on exchange rates twice, but it was still cheaper than the 550 Euro I would've been paying otherwise.

I wish I had a cool story as to what the mafia was using my apartment for, but I do not. Truth is, had Sara not told me they were using it, I would never have known. Whatever they did, they cleaned up after themselves. When I came home from work I'd check for blood or drug residue – any proof that someone had been there. Nothing. It was nice to know I was associating with clean gangsters, if nothing else. With Sara as my go-between, I never had to come face-to-face with any of them.

Until I lost my job and couldn't pay them.

With so many English teachers descending upon Prague to find work, my employer realized they could cut the pay of their teachers in half and still maintain an adequate supply of instructors. I organized a small group of teachers to strike, protesting our wage cuts. Bad move.

We were replaced before a single class was interrupted, leaving all 10 of us without jobs. Making matters worse, my last private lesson student, Paxon, had just returned to Germany, leaving me with no money coming in.

The teaching market in Prague was saturated. In the year I'd been there, wages were more than halved, with spoiled rich kids moving in to take our jobs, mommy and daddy back home footing the bill, using the pay they received from teaching on beer and prostitutes. Good for Sara, bad for me. I decided it'd be best to return to California.

But I had a problem.

I had enough money to buy a plane ticket home and nothing else. My flight left in 3 weeks, but I only had enough patches to last me 2 weeks.

Like usual, I devised a plan, and as always, it ended up completely fucking me in the end.

The mafia usually gave me a 1-week grace period to pay Sara for my patches. If I timed it just right, I could get the patches and then bounce out of Prague with no one noticing. Or so I thought.

The day before my flight left, Sara stopped by, unannounced, overcoat covering lingerie, like she often did, to do coke and watch *Saved by the Bell*. I had most of my things packed up, tripping off Sara's common sense.

"Jason, you go?"

"Uhh... yeah, but not for a few days."

She looked worried. "Jason, you must pay first," begged Sara.

Looking back, I realize that they probably were going to hold Sara accountable for any of my debts, since she was my go-between. But a drug addict really doesn't give a shit about anybody else's fate, friend or not.

Shit, I'd burned my family, my own blood. You think I thought twice about burning a Russian prostitute?

"Yes, of course I'll pay," I lied. "I leave on Saturday, so I will pay you on Friday."

It was Monday, but I wanted to leave myself some breathing room.

As I talked, I walked downstairs to grab my laptop. When I came back up, still talking, Sara was gone.

Weird, but Sara often did weird shit, so I didn't think much of it. I continued gathering my things into a neat, little pile in the middle of my living room for the next hour. Upon finishing, I lay down on my couch and threw on a DVD to relax since I didn't even have enough money to go out for my last night in Prague.

Suddenly, I was hit with a wave of anxiety and panic.

Sitting on the table by the door, right where Sara was standing when I went downstairs, was my plane ticket. On my ticket, the date and time of my actual departure, printed in large, black letters.

Fuck.

I jumped up and quickly grabbed my luggage and passport just as I heard someone at my front door. I grabbed what I could – which wasn't much – and ran downstairs, climbing out of a window that faced the garden of my apartment complex. All I had time to take was my small luggage – coincidentally, the luggage with the patches in it – and my passport. I had to leave everything else, including most of my clothes, in the apartment.

I snuck around to the front to check if there was someone watching, which there was not. Peeking inside the front window, I watched as Sara led the man through my apartment and pointed out anything that was of any value.

Once again, I was the victim.

How could Sara turn on me like that? I thought we were friends! This bitch sold me out!

Never mind the fact that I completely sold her out by trying to walk out on my debt to her mafia friends. Never mind the fact that I lied to her about when I left and tried to completely fuck her over. Never mind the fact that I even involved myself in this weird prostitute-mafia triangle just so I could get my drugs. I was the victim. Poor me. How could this happen to me? I was innocent and now Sara was selling me out to protect herself? The nerve of this chick! I never thought a Russian prostitute would sell me out like this.

"Never trust a Russian prostitute," I told myself, probably while she thought, "Never trust an American drug addict."

While frozen rain pelted me in the face and my clothes became soaked in mud, I watched through the window in the dark as Sara led the man in the black skullcap through my apartment. He walked through my home as if he were shopping, pointing things out for Sara to grab. My DVD player, CD player, all of my DVDs and CDs, my television, coffee maker, microwave, shit that wasn't even mine but came with the apartment. They made a pile in the middle of my living room, coupled with the pile I had made earlier, until the man was satisfied. Before leaving, I watched Sara turn back, grabbing one more thing: my *Saved by the Bell* DVDs. Finally, the two of them left my apartment together, not even turning off the light.

There was no way I was going back inside. I don't know if they set a trap for me to return or were sending in guys to carry everything out, but I wasn't going to stick around to find out. I took my small bag and passport, getting the fuck out of the neighborhood without looking back.

I slept that night in the subway station until the trains started running, at which point I took the subway to the bus, which took me to the airport. I was hyper-paranoid, walking through the airport with my head down, just trying to make it to the security gate. Any sudden movement made me jump. Looking back, it's comical. At the time, it was frightening.

I made it to my flight and returned to California with a Fentanyl habit that had just begun taking control of the ever-increasing chaos I called my life.

"You see what I'm talking about? We're victims, man. There you were, in a situation involving the mafia, a Russian prostitute, and Schedule II narcotics, and yet you felt victimized," said my sponsor, shaking his head, laughing.

"Dude, that shit was intense!" I protested.

"I'm sure it was," he agreed. "But who, ultimately, put you in that situation?"

His line of thinking was starting to sink in, and I began seeing my part in all of the chaos I'd spread throughout the years. The sudden absorption of blame was intense, leaving me with more emotions than I knew how to handle. I was ashamed, felt guilty, angry, remorseful, overwhelmed. But the fact that I had someone right next to me to help me through it kept me from doing what I normally would do in this situation: get high until those feelings went away. Knowing he'd been right where I was gave me a comfort I otherwise would have never felt in this situation.

"You were pulling 'geographics,' man. We've all done it," he explained. "You were dying inside, going crazy, but working on that shit is hard. Working on yourself is hard. So you did what so many of us have done – you tried running away from your problems, like a child," he said, his hand on my shoulder, watching as my brain raced from one emotion to the other.

"What happened after you got back home," my sponsor asked.

"I got hired teaching high school."

"No shit?"

"Yeah, I taught for 3 years: US History, Gov-Econ, Psychology. Social Science."

"How'd that work out?" he asked, his curiosity seemingly genuine.

"Actually, really well for a while. I loved it. In the classroom I felt comfortable, got along well with the kids."

"Were you using?"

"Yep. But it was like in Prague. I applied, interviewed, and was hired when I was high. That was the only 'me' they knew."

"So they never knew?"

"No. But it started getting really bad. I was on the Fentanyl and about 50 Norco a day, and I wasn't getting high. Not even a little high. I needed that just to not be sick."

"Ugh, I've been there. I don't miss it," he said, looking down, remembering. "That's a fucked up feeling when you can't get high anymore."

"I stopped with the Soma and Xanax, because I was noticeably different on those. But with the Fentanyl and Norco, nobody could really tell. Then it all changed."

"What do you mean?"

"Depression," I said with disdain. "That fucking depression.

It's like my brain got overloaded with chemicals and just shut down completely."

"Depression?"

"Yeah. Empty, bottomless, numb, gray, depression," I told him, staring once again at a grazing horse in the distance.

"How'd you get out of it?" he pressed.

"The jailers in Mexico snapped me out of it."

CHAPTER 6.

TIJUANA JAIL

This is not what I had planned for my life, to be kicking Fentanyl by myself, alone, with no say in the matter. The freedom to make the choice to get clean on my own was gone. Woosh, just like that. The Mexican penal system decided it was going to make that choice for me–I was going to kick in a Tijuana jail cell.

The doctor in Prague was right – Fentanyl was indeed stronger than heroin, and 50–100 times more potent than morphine. Prior to my incarceration, I was a zombie, sucking the drug from a patch that was supposed to go on my skin, which landed me in this world of concrete the Mexicans called a jail.

The days of steering my way out of drug-addict-tailspins were over. It was time for a crash.

About a year prior to hearing the guards yell out "Yayson Smeet" each morning so they could wake me up and beat the shit out of me, I woke up one day in my Northern California home and couldn't feel. Anything. Nothing. My world had gone gray overnight, a complete and total mental breakdown that I kept a secret. I left my job teaching high school and spent a year lying on a couch.

An entire year of nothing.

I remember thinking about taking the trash out, and the energy that would take. I didn't have it. You might as well have told me to go run a 10K. Walking outside was a task I was not up for.

It was crazy.

I had always assumed depression was sadness, simply the opposite of being happy. I learned that, for me, depression was nothingness. Sadness, in fact, would have been a welcome feeling, in that it would have at least been a feeling. Instead I was in a deeply depressed land of no emotion, no feeling, no heart, no ambition, no strength.

Family would stop by asking what was wrong and I'd tell them I was fine, that the homeless look was in fashion, to leave me alone, to please quit staring at my blacked-out windows. My home went into foreclosure because paying my mortgage required too much effort.

Don't get me wrong, I had the money. I'm talking about the act of getting out a checkbook, writing a check and placing it into an envelope—I couldn't do it. I lacked the energy.

I told myself that I didn't know what was wrong, but I was lying. I knew exactly what it was: It was those fucking Fentanyl patches. I'd been on them for more than half a decade by this point, in combination with Norco and sporadic Xanax abuse, Dr. Frankenstein aka Dr. Maven's monster, pieced together with narcotics and benzodiazepines. Unwittingly, I'd pushed my brain to a chemically-induced point that it couldn't handle. So it said "fuck it" and shut down completely, leaving me on a couch without enough energy to pick up a pen and write a check.

It's a strange thing to know the source of your misery

but be too afraid to remove it from your life. Lying on my couch, I knew exactly what the problem was. I was like a battered wife, beaten into submission and wanting to leave but too afraid to face the world alone.

One day while lying down, not doing shit in typically-depressed fashion, I was watching *Intervention* on A&E. *Intervention* is one of those cable shows that tricks a drug addict into thinking that for some reason, the network has to decided to devote lots of money to doing a documentary on their pathetic, drug-addicted life for no good reason.

In reality, it's a set-up with the family staging an intervention, but only after the true extent of depravity that is their life is revealed for the world to see. The addict eventually succumbs to their pressure, usually after mommy or daddy threatens to cut them off financially, giving you a warm feeling inside because this drug addict is going to get the help that he or she needs. They usually flash forward, showing the addict 60 days into their treatment, looking healthy and happy, far from the twisted-wreck-of-a-human you just watched deteriorate before your eyes for 56 minutes.

"Johnny spent 86 days at xxxx Treatment Center."

You feel real good about the situation, genuinely happy that Johnny finally got his shit together.

That is, until they flash on the screen at the end:

"Johnny left rehab after 80 days, stayed clean for two weeks, and then relapsed. He currently lives on the streets of Portland."

It leaves you with a real *what the fuck?* feeling when it's over and done with.

Anyway, there was a guy on one of these *Intervention* episodes who put the patches in his cheek instead of on his skin, since that let him absorb the entire dose of the patch all at once through the mucus membranes of his mouth, which absorb substances much more quickly and efficiently than does the skin.

You know you're a drug addict when you watch a show like *Intervention* and your only take away is, *shit, I never thought of doing drugs like that.*

I decided to skip the second half of the episode and try this method for myself. Pulling a patch out of its packaging, I peeled it away from the thin plastic that it comes attached to, slid it inside of my left cheek, and waited.

It took about 30 seconds, and when it hit, it hit hard.

Woooooosh.

Euphoria. Instant Euphoria.

For the first time in a year, I FELT SOMETHING. Sure, the high was great. But I was just relieved to be able to feel again. I had energy. I could eat. I could leave the house. I could interact with people again. I had life.

I should have watched the second half of that *Intervention* episode.

The problem with doing Fentanyl patches orally, I'd soon find out, is the patches don't last. A patch that is prescribed to last two days on your skin instead lasts only four hours in your mouth.

Those fuckers at *Intervention* failed to tell me this.

Running through four to five patches a day meant I ran out of my prescription early. Very early. And these weren't like pills that I could scam out of some Urgent Care facility at will. These were Schedule II narcotics, meaning the DEA got copies of each prescription, making them nearly impossible to get from multiple doctors without getting caught up by the feds.

It was at this time I got a call from Paxon, the German

business-English student of mine from Prague who had an odd affinity for root beer floats and Robbie Williams. Those days of living in Prague seemed forever ago, when in reality it had only been 3 years. I was aging by a different standard than the traditional calendar.

"Hey, Jason! How are you?"

I skipped over the living on a couch for a year and sucking on Fentanyl patches part.

"I'm good man, what's up?"

"My friend Toni is in California right now, traveling around. He really wants to go to Mexico and asked me if I knew anyone who could take him."

Ding, ding, ding.

Mexico. The den of all things chemical. You can get anything in Mexico. Remember that feeling of walking into a Toys 'R' Us as a kid? That's what it feels like for a drug addict walking into a Mexican pharmacy. Or farmacia. Whatever.

I've often heard stories about the "Donkey Show" in Mexico, which is, apparently a girl getting romantic with a donkey. The story is thrown around so loosely, as if it's perfectly acceptable to watch a donkey fuck a human. But if I were to travel down with a group on their way to see a donkey show and tell them, "Hey, I'm gonna hit up the farmacia to get some drugs and get high while you guys go watch a person fuck a donkey," I'm sure somebody would pull me aside, tell me that I'm fucked up, that I need help. I should see a counselor. That there are places for people like me to get the help I need.

Society is funny like that.

Crossing over the border with Toni in San Diego at the San Ysidro crossing, I felt free. Free from the DEA's oversight, free from all responsibility, free from the family and friends I was forcing to watch me deteriorate. It was liberating in a really sick sense.

We drove to Rosarito Beach, where we got a room at the Rosarito Beach Hotel. I knew better than to try and get Fentanyl from a farmacia directly. Even for Mexico, that was a heavy order. Fentanyl and OxyContin were two drugs the Mexicans were more careful with, and I was just some gringo off the street. I needed someone on the inside.

While Toni slept, I approached the guy cleaning the hotel pool one morning as he used a skimmer to get bugs off the surface.

"Hey man, do you speak English?"

He just looked at me blankly, shaking his head no.

"You wanna make $50 dollars?"

Suddenly he spoke English.

"You know anybody who works at a farmacia?"

He just nodded. "My tia."

Perfect.

I paid him $50 to gather a little intel. I needed to know how many I could get, what strength, how much. The basics.

He reported back, and it was a jackpot: Whatever I wanted, however many I wanted, for dirt cheap.

It was a true "Eureka!" moment, what I imagine Americans felt in 1849 as they struck gold for the first time. Coincidentally, leading us to take California from Mexico.

I handed him a wad of cash and followed him from a distance to his aunt's farmacia. I paid a teenager $5 to stand behind the building and yell if anyone came out the back, just to make sure I didn't get ripped off. For five minutes I waited, eyes jumping back and forth, watching for policia. Finally, the pool cleaner exited the building with a bag of 100-microgram Fentanyl patches and a few boxes of blue 1 mg Xanax tablets.

Easy-peezy.

After five days in Rosarito, where Visa and Mastercard generously funded my drug habit, we loaded up the car to come home. The pool-cleaning guy made one last trip for me the morning we left, so I was stocked up. I was all lined up for a few months of personal drug-consumption.

Unfortunately, the Mexicans would see it as trafficking.

Getting into Mexico is easy. Getting out, not so much. Crossing back into San Diego from Tijuana you sit in a line of cars just waiting, inching your way toward the giant American flag waiting just on the other side. There are people who roam the aisles of cars, selling various things: Soccer jerseys, Virgin Marys, Chicklets, piñatas, churros.

All of a sudden there was a knock on the backseat window, passenger side. Standing there was a woman, dressed provocatively, doing her best to look seductive. Seeing that she wasn't carrying anything to sell, I assumed she was selling herself.

"No, gracias," I said, mouthing the words so she could read my lips.

She walked to the front seat, where Toni was sitting.

Knock, knock, knock. She bent over, looking inside the car, cleavage in abundance.

"NO GRACIAS," I yelled. I cracked the window, and said it again. "Fuck off!"

Reaching over, she opened the rear passenger-side door. I lost it.

"No quiero una puta!" I yelled. *I don't want a whore.*

This lady snapped and started screaming at the top of

her lungs. Every passenger of every car in the vicinity was looking our way. She caught the attention of a police officer standing off to the side of the road. As he walked over, I closed my eyes, realizing the varying degrees to which I was totally fucked.

"What is going on?" the officer asked in English.

"I don't know, man. This lady..." and she cut me off, speaking to the officer in rapid-fire Spanish. I'm not sure what she said, but whatever it was, it caused the officer to ask me to turn off the car and step outside of the vehicle.

With my hands on the hood, the officer patted me down, where he found patch, after patch, after patch. I was wearing cargo shorts, and every pocket was stuffed full of them.

Handcuffing me, he put me into the back of a white Toyota pick-up truck. There's no comfortable way to sit with handcuffs on, and having to sit in the back of a pick-up just added to the hurt. The cuffs tightened with every bump and turn.

He told Toni to follow him. Sitting with my back against the cab of the truck, I stared at Toni, who tailed us closely. Toni had no idea of my exploits while we were in Mexico. This poor fucking German tourist just got sucked into the chaos that my life was becoming.

The truck drove away from the bustle of Tijuana, eventually pulling off at a stone building that was not near anything. He took my cuffs off, almost apologetically.

"Ok, you must pay a fine for this. Five hundred dollars and you go home," he said, looking at both of us.

"Five hundred dollars? Are you serious? We don't have five hundred dollars," I told him, half-considering just bolting and taking my chances in a chase through the desert.

"No," he said, seeming annoyed. "Five hundred you," and he pointed to me, "and five hundred you," he said pointing at Toni.

"A THOUSAND DOLLARS?" I asked, incredulously.

The Mexican just smiled and nodded his head.

Without thinking, I opened my mouth and said something that I wanted to take back but could not.

"FUCK YOU," I yelled, immediately regretting it.

The Mexican was smiling no more.

"You," he said, pointing to Toni, "go home." Shit got serious, quickly. He cuffed my hands behind my back again and walked me toward the passenger side of the truck. I looked back at Toni who had a look on his face that begged for answers to what was happening. I had none. None that I was willing to give him, at least.

The officer opened the passenger door and placed his hand on the back of my neck. I assumed he was letting me ride shotgun this time, making sure I wouldn't bump my head as I got in.

I was wrong.

Grabbing me by the back of the hair, he pulled back and slammed my forehead into the frame of the truck above the door.

I was dazed and fell to my knees. Reflexes forced me to try and put my hands in front of me, which tightened the cuffs to the point that they were cutting into my hands. I could feel blood dripping off of my left wrist. He swung and hit me on the head behind my right ear, turning me around and flat on my ass. I looked up, confused with my head writhing in pain, just in time to see his right hand cocked back before he swung again, hitting me under my left eye. I could feel blood gushing from my left cheek, dripping down my chin.

Then, everything went black. When I woke up, I was lying on my stomach in a Tijuana Jail cell. I lifted my head up just long enough to see that there was another white guy in the cell with me.

"Aye man, are you all right?" he asked.

When I blinked I could feel throbbing in my cheek, so I decided to keep my eyes closed. And when I tried to talk, my jaw hurt, so I decided to keep my mouth closed.

I was anything but "all right."

The guards had taken the Fentanyl patches off of my stomach, and emptied my pockets of their contents.

The pain I felt from the punches didn't come close to the pain I was about to endure in the coming days.

Before you judge–assuming it's not too late–allow me to explain something. Drug addiction is a love affair, pure and simple. It's hot, and passionate, and seductive, and engrossing. It's captivating, in that it makes an addict think about the drug non-stop, never content because you know what you have won't last, regardless of the size of the most recent score. Maintaining an addiction is a game of chess, ever contemplating the NEXT move, the NEXT score, for fear that when what you have is gone, you'll be without.

Oh, God, that fear.

Being without means getting sick. And getting sick is something that, short of being locked up, you just won't let happen.

Well, I was locked up.

In jail.

In Tijuana.

The cell was beige, with two metal beds, angled chains holding one above the other. At the ends of the beds was what, I suppose, could be considered a toilet. The floor angled into a hole in the ground.

No toilet seat. No toilet paper. No toilet. Just a hole.

When I opened my eyes the second time, my cellmate was gone. I'm not sure he was ever there in the first place. Sitting up, my head throbbing, I surveyed the scene. It didn't look good. My cell faced a long, narrow hallway, with cells on the opposite side facing me. Those cells were packed with inmates, all in for various crimes, mainly drugs and alcohol. I was the only white guy.

"Good morning!" one guy shouted, in accented English, as he laughed. "Man, they fucked you up good!"

I just smiled. Ironically, it was the only facial expression I could make that didn't hurt.

I was still wearing the clothes I was arrested in: Cargo shorts, T-shirt, and a pair of white and black Adidas with the laces removed so I wouldn't hang myself. The jail was hot and filled with artificial light, making it impossible to know if it was day or night. Realizing my predicament, I figured I'd have at least a few days without getting sick because I'd put a few Fentanyl patches on my stomach that morning.

Reaching under my shirt to make sure I'd be OK—something you do constantly when you're wearing the patches—I felt nothing. I felt skin where patches should have been, only a sticky residue left behind.

I had nothing. Realizing the guards had taken them off of me, I panicked.

Jumping off my top bunk, I called for a guard. "Hey, man, I need a doctor. Necessito un doctor. Hello?"

What appeared could have been a casting for a bad movie. Overweight guard, thick, bushy, black mustache, handcuffs dangling, spinning a nightstick around in his hand.

"You need doctor?" he asked, arching his eyebrows.

"Yes, PLEASE. Por Favor. Si."

He motioned for me to turn around and put my hands behind my back. I stuck my hands through a slot in the bars, and he placed the cuffs on me. I turned around, facing him, eye-to-eye, through the bars.

He pulled a clipboard from a slot on the wall and read.

"Yay-son Smeet." And then looked at me, as if awaiting confirmation.

This was no time to dispute pronunciation.

I nodded my head, "Si."

Placing the clipboard back in its slot, he opened the cell door. I stepped forward, thinking we'd be walking somewhere. He placed a hand on my chest with more strength than I'd anticipated, forcing me to stumble back. I looked at him, slightly confused. Reaching back, he hit me with an uppercut to the stomach with much more force than someone his size should've been able to produce. His punch dropped me to my knees, taking all the air out of my lungs. I knelt with my chin on the lower bunk, gasping, trying to catch my breath.

The prisoners on the other side just watched, silently.

That was all.

He took the handcuffs off of my wrists, which were rubbed completely raw by this point, casually left the cell, turned around, locked it, and walked off, swinging his nightstick as if nothing happened.

Lying down on my back, I outstretched my arms above my head, letting oxygen slowly return to my body. From my cell floor I stared at the ceiling, and it stared back. I realized I was going to have to do this and it wasn't going to be pleasant.

It's a sad state to contemplate suicide from the deepest part of your being, only to realize you don't have the means to carry it out. Which only left one alternative: Severe withdrawal.

When you start to kick opiates, the mental anguish sets in before the physical. The anticipation of the withdrawal is actually its first stage, where anguish commences. Misery's coming-out-party. The only thing worse than a journey through hell is knowing that you're about to go on a journey through hell.

Everything about withdrawal is the complete opposite of the high. As good as you feel on opiates is as bad as you feel coming off of them. I've heard people compare detox to the flu, which is comical. When was the last time you had a flu that made you contemplate suicide?

Detox is your body fighting like hell to get back to normal, while your brain fights like hell to stay high. You're simply caught in the middle, an innocent bystander whose innocence was lost a long time ago.

That feeling of warm water running through your veins that you get when high—now it's ice cold and screams at you, relentlessly. Every vein in your body burns. Your skin hurts. That's right, your fucking skin hurts. You're vomiting up something awful and your joints feel like they're made of cold steel. You're sneezing and your eyes feel like they're going to burn out of their sockets while pumping out a seemingly endless amount of tears.

You're yawning, regardless of the fact that sleep is the last thing you're going to get. It's almost like your brain is teasing you with the things it would do for you, if you would only just find a way to get high.

I lay myself on the bottom bunk, which had no mattress or pillow or blanket. The metal bed was cold to the touch as I tried to dig my face into it as hard as I could, knees to my chest, curled up, trying to redirect the pain to other parts of my body. I was lying in the fetal position the first time the guards did their morning roll call. That's the only way I knew it was morning.

I was curled up, facing the wall of the cell beneath the shadow of the top bunk.

"Yay-son Smeet?"

I just lay there, noticeably aggravating the guard. I wasn't sure what I was supposed to do in response, but it was obviously different than what I was doing.

"YAY-SON SMEET?" He raised his voice.

When you're kicking, it doesn't take much to piss you off. Everybody is an enemy because your sole desire is to get high, and anybody offering anything but that is a fucking nuisance.

"Yes, I'm right here. Jesus. There's one fucking white guy in this whole place. Let's use some deductive reasoning skills to figure out if "Yay-son" is here."

I couldn't see the guard's face because I was facing the wall, but I heard him enter, and I felt him grab the back of my T-shirt. He pulled, dragging me out from under the top bunk. He didn't even bother cuffing me because I was obviously in no condition to fight back. He turned me around so I was sitting on the bunk, facing him, and hit me under my left eye with a right cross–the exact same spot the cop who arrested me had hit me. My head snapped back into the metal side of the top bunk, which hurt much more than the punch did. I put my hands over my head and lay back down. I heard the guard exit, lock the cage, and continue down the line of his roll call.

Kicking at home is bad, but not this bad. At home you know in the back of your mind you can make a phone call, visit a doctor, pull the old "Ibuprofen hurts my stomach" bullshit, and get what you need. But this was a different kind of kick. My brain knew this was it--there was no phone call to make, no doctor to visit, no dealer to call. I mean, shit, where was I going to go?

The worst part about getting through day one was knowing that there would be a day two. Day two was vomiting and diarrhea. With a hole in the ground and no toilet paper. Thankfully, I arrived wearing long socks.

Losing this much fluid meant I needed to put something back in to feel any relief. But that was, shall we say, a problem.

Every morning, one of the inmates was tasked with mopping up the spit and vomit and piss and shit and whatever else found its way onto the floor of the jail. As they went by with the mop it became hard to breathe. My throat closed up, but I thought that was just part of the detox. I noticed, however, the inmates across from me coughing as well. On day two the same thing happened. It made me gag and dry heave, but in a different key than my withdrawal gags and dry heaves.

A man who introduced himself as Jorge and spoke pretty good English looked at me from his cell which was directly across from mine.

"Is lye," he said, matter-of-factly.

"Lye?"

"Si. Is lye," he motioned to his throat. "Is hot."

My throat was burning and I needed a drink, but there was no water in the cell.

"Do we get water?" I asked, slowly emerging from my bottom-bunk cavern.

"Si." He grabbed a large McDonalds plastic cup that was perched in the upper-left hand side of his cell. I looked up and saw that I had one in my cell as well.

I was confused. "Where do we fill it?"

Jorge yelled in Spanish at the guy mopping the floor to come back. Handing over the cup, the guy with the mop bucket dipped the plastic cup into the mop bucket and passed it back to Jorge.

I looked on, stunned. Frozen. Speechless.

Jorge gave me a look that asked, *Do you know where you're at, motherfucker?*

My body was screaming for water. I was dehydrated, vomiting, and sweating because the jail was humid.

The man holding the mop looked at me, waiting to see if I had a cup for him to fill before he could go on his way. Broken, dried blood on my forehead and face, I handed him my plastic McDonalds cup. He handed it back to me, full.

I drank from it. It burned, but it went down. I drank some more.

I'm not sure what day it was because time wasn't really broken into days in that jail. It was broken down into segments between roll calls. We were never let outside, never allowed to shower, and all we ate were plates of rice and bread. With our meals we were allowed water that wasn't mop water.

It was a day when my body was beginning to feel a little better, so it had to have been more than three days. Day three is the detox climax, where you know that it's not going to get any worse than that. I was losing my voice from drinking lye-laced water, but I could feel life starting to enter my body. I could stand up, walk around, and only occasionally have to throw up.

That morning when the guard walked by I asked if I could talk to the US consulate. Before he cuffed me and hit me in the stomach, however, he flashed a look of concern. That was the first sign that something was amiss.

My stomach and chest were bruised, but the punches began to get redundant. They kept hitting me in the same spots, which by that point were totally numb. I felt an element of strength that I hadn't felt before, and the stronger I felt, the more confident I felt pushing the issue.

"Hey," I barked at the next guard that walked by a few hours later. "I want to talk to a consulate representative." He looked at me sideways, cocked his head back, began to open my cage, but decided instead to re-lock it and scurry off to some part of the jail that I was unable to see.

I began to identify the guards by how they beat me. There were three different guards. The skinny one with the goatee liked to hit me in the face, so I didn't push it with him. I just waited until his shift was over. The two other guards, both with bushy mustaches, would hit me in the stomach and chest, which I could deal with, so I started insisting on talking to someone from my consulate when they were on duty.

I began to feel more mental strength. I knew that were I not cuffed I could handle both of these guys. Knowing this gave me the will to endure. Knowing that they knew this made me feel even stronger. On day one they could drop me with one shot. I liked knowing that as days passed, it took more and more punches to drop me to my knees. I liked, even more, knowing that they knew this as well.

One shift they called my name, but it wasn't during roll call. "Yay-son Smeet?" It wasn't a guard. He was a gentle-looking older man with a long, straggly, gray goatee wearing a white medical coat.

"Si," I said, hopping off of my bottom bunk.

"Come with me," and he motioned for a guard to unlock my cell.

After they cuffed me I followed him down the line of cells, overflowing with people, making me question why I'd been alone the whole time. Finally I got to see what the rest of the jail looked like, since I was unconscious when I came in.

The man led me to a small, smoke-stained office with wooden floors. I sat down on a chair, uncomfortably, since there was still no good way to sit down with handcuffs on.

He looked at me and tilted his head back, leaning back in his chair. "I'd ask you how you are doing, but we both know the answer to that."

We both laughed. It felt good to laugh.

"Why do you speak English so well?" I asked him out of curiosity.

With a look of pride he stated, "I went to San Diego State for undergraduate studies."

"No shit? That was the first school that ever recruited me to play football for them," I told him, doing my best to match his level of pride.

"You played American football? You look like it. You look strong, which, just so you know, is why the guards beat you so often. It makes them feel better about themselves," he smiled.

I didn't know who this guy was, but I liked him.

"Jason, you concern me. That was a lot of Fentanyl they caught you with. Why do you take so much?"

Nobody had ever asked me that question before.

"I had back surgery, and it just sort of got out of control," I explained. Strangely, in this surreal environment surrounded by decrepit conditions, I was actually being honest with somebody about my addiction for the first time in my life.

He scooted his chair forward and looked at me. "Jason, I'm the doctor for the jail, and I'm going to issue your release on medical conditions. Because of the withdrawal I witnessed you go through, I've determined that the Fentanyl you were caught with was for yourself, not for sales. But I want you to promise me that when you get home you will get help."

"I promise," I blurted out immediately, not really sure if I meant it or not.

"You have to promise me you will be finished with this Fentanyl," he said, waiting for my response.

"I promise."

He looked me in my eyes until he believed me.

"OK, follow me," he said, standing up, opening his office door, and leading me toward what looked to be the processing area.

The doctor handed some paperwork to a guard I didn't recognize. The guard motioned for me to turn around and took the handcuffs off of my wrists, then looked at the paperwork one last time. "Yay-son Smeet?" I prayed that was the last time I would hear that.

"Si," I nodded.

Opening a wide, steel door that led out into a humid waiting room, the guard handed me my drivers license and that was it. It seemed a very anti-climactic finish to the week.

No wallet. No phone. Filthy clothes. A bruised body. A bloodied face. And Adidas with no shoelaces.

It was like a really fucked up Run DMC video.

I left the jail with no physical addiction to any drug. I'd gone through the most horrific kick of my life, in the most disgusting of conditions, in what amounted to a third-world jail. This was a chance to start anew. Free from addiction, free from Fentanyl, free from doctors. This was my chance.

I hitched a ride into town with a guy who was there to pay a traffic ticket. I had him drop me off at a bank, where I went inside and wired myself $100 from my savings account. It was my last $100, since the police had spent the entire duration of my incarceration draining my checking account and maxing out my credit cards.

Leaving the bank with the last $100 to my name, I walked toward the border. At a gas station I bought a giant bottle of water and a large Arizona Iced Green Tea. I finished both drinks before I got to the counter.

This left me $98 to get home. I would need this money to get from the border at San Ysidro to the airport, where I had a ticketless reservation with Southwest. It wasn't much, but it would be enough.

As I walked past the vehicles waiting in the same line of cars where I'd been arrested, there were signs everywhere. "Farmacia." "Discount Drugs." "Generic Prices."

Don't do it, Jason. Be strong.

As I walked by, pharmaceutical carnival-barkers stood outside their respective pharmacies, inviting me to come in.

"You want drugs? Steroids? Sudafed? Amphetamines?"
No thanks. Not my thing.
I kept walking, passing another farmacia.
"Cialis? Viagra?"
Viagra, what? Fuck you.
"You want Ritalin? Adderall?"
Just keep walking Jason. Just keep walking. You got this. You're almost there.
"Xanax? Valium?"
My ears perked up, like when a dog hears a siren in the distance, and the $98 in my pocket got heavier.
"Vicodin? Norco? Soma?"
All of a sudden, the distance to the border seemed entirely too far to walk un-medicated.
"You have Norco?" I asked the man, like a fish toying with bait.
"Si, si. Come in," he said, setting the hook as he opened the door for me.
"How can I help you?" asked the old man behind the counter, knowing good-and-goddamn well what I was after before I even said it.
"Do you have Fentanyl?" I asked, in a defeated tone. Pool-cleaning guy was nowhere to be found, but I figured I'd give it a shot. A drug-addict Hail Mary.
He looked at the man working the door who nodded his head and locked the door.
"Si, I have it, but this is very strong medication, señor. How much do you need?"
Glaring at the man behind the counter, I paused, thinking about the entire last week and how if I gave in now, I'd just have to eventually do it all over again. My chest was bruised to the point where it hurt to breathe and I could feel the dried blood on my face. I hated this

fucking drug for what it had done to me. To my core, I hated it.

I looked him dead in the eyes.

"How much can $98 get me?"

———

"If you ever in your life start to question whether or not you're a drug addict," my sponsor said, deadpan serious, "I want you to remember this story."

We sat in silence for what seemed like forever, replaying the pure insanity that I'd just described.

"There's going to be a point in your recovery," he continued, "when things will start going well for you. You'll start to get a life back, family, friends, career, all of it. All of those things will undoubtedly happen for you at some point if you stay clean. And when that happens, you'll start to question whether or not you're still an addict. You'll start to think, 'I bet I could do drugs responsibly now,' 'I can drink responsibly now,' whatever. It will happen."

And he paused, looking at me.

"And when it does, I want you to remember this story."

I sat, silently.

"You mean I never get to be like that asshole in the Malibu Passages commercial, claiming 'I used to be a drug addict. Now I'm not.'?" I asked.

We laughed, which felt good. I needed to smile.

"You can try it," he said. "But I don't recommend it."

Describing the transition to my sponsor like this, chronologically, allowed me to see for the first time just how insane the transition was.

"It's crazy. From that first time next to the Sierra College

library to a jail cell in Mexico was a decade of my life. A fucking decade, gone," I said, realizing that I hurt myself just as much, if not more, than anybody else.

"Well, the bad news is you can't change the past. That shit's in stone and isn't going anywhere. The past is the past."

"How am I supposed to move on when I can't change the past?" I asked him.

He thought long and hard, as if he was staring back into his own years of death and destruction.

"It's tough," he said, nodding his head. "I won't lie. But if you just do what's right, eventually you'll have a new past, one you can be proud of."

I wanted to get up and leave when I heard this. What he was describing sounded like it took a long time, and patience wasn't a virtue I'd grown accustomed to.

As a drug addict, I want instant gratification. Now. Right now. Not only am I impatient, but I'm a procrastinator, making me the ultimate asshole, because I want what I want, when I want it, but when YOU want it, I'm going to wait until the last possible second.

Because I'm THAT fucking important.

It makes sense when you think about it. Drugs work right now. There's no effort required to change the way we feel once the chemicals enter our bloodstream. We do the drugs and feel the results immediately. I'm not aware of any drug that requires years of hard work and self-reflection before taking effect. We take drugs to wake up, drugs to go to sleep, drugs to feel up, drugs to feel down, drugs that make us happy, drugs that depress us. If there's an emotion we're after, there is a drug to bring us there. So getting clean and realizing it will take years to repair some of the damage we've caused can be a little much.

But the drugs had stopped working for me, and suicide didn't work, so this was my only option.

"That would've been the bottom for a lot of people," my sponsor said.

"I wish I could say it was."

"Why wasn't it?"

"Because I wasn't done. I wasn't ready," I tried to explain. "I just wasn't done – there's no other real explanation for it."

"Let me guess," he joked, "you eased up on the drugs and started taking them responsibly."

All we could do was laugh.

"That would've saved me a lot of money in court fees," I said, still laughing.

CHAPTER 7.

MAPLE SYRUP, ICE HOCKEY, & HAGGIS

2008 was an ugly year. Brutal. The depression leading up to my incarceration in Tijuana Jail broke me down, and the jailers in Tijuana broke my spirit. I medicated that hurt, that pain, that sinister feeling of feeling, the only way I knew how: Fentanyl, liquid-morphine, and Xanax.

It worked. Until, once again, it didn't. The month after getting out of jail in Mexico, I started grad school at Cal Poly, San Luis Obispo. I figured moving further down the coast would help. I was wrong–my first month there, I picked up two DUIs in one night, along with a public-intoxication charge for (allegedly) knocking on my neighbor's door and asking to use her phone. When she said no, I (allegedly) took the slipper off of her foot and tried to make a phone call on it.

Makin' mamma proud.

I say "allegedly" not for legal reasons; that shit's on my official record and going nowhere. I say "allegedly" because I don't remember any of it. Not a single thing.

The word spiral doesn't adequately capture the state I was in. The Fentanyl and liquid-morphine, which I got turned onto by an aunt (doing her part in upholding

Smith family traditions), didn't get me high anymore. They just kept me from being sick. As a drug addict, this is a fucked up situation to find yourself in. It's like the drugs have turned on you, refusing to hold up their end of the bargain, refusing to show their gratitude for the dirty, conniving, manipulative, inhumane shit you had to do to get your hands on them. No matter how much I did, I couldn't get high.

I went from chasing a high to running from a detox.

The Xanax, on the other hand, did its part and did it well. Xanax, a benzodiazepine, is an anti-anxiety drug. Had I followed the directions on the label, it would have calmed my nerves and helped me relax. But I never followed the directions on the label. Fuck the label, I wanted to get high. I have no idea why they were prescribed to me, because I've never suffered from anxiety. But they were prescribed, and, by God, I took them.

When taken in excess, and/or chopped up and snorted, Xanax completely changed my personality. I'm normally a very laid-back, relaxed person. Xanax altered me to the core. I'd get aggressive, confrontational, 'fuck-you-you-wanna-fight' in the grocery store aisle. I became a monster. To make matters worse, the more I'd take, the more I'd want, meaning I would take seven or eight 1mg tablets a day and go on these three or four day blackouts. I would wake up with cuts and bruises all over my face and body from falling down and have to backtrack using text messages, which were complete gibberish, and receipts from my pockets. It was like that movie *Memento* but way more fucked up and pathetic.

On one of these blackouts I was arrested for a DUI. They got me for driving on Fentanyl and Xanax, and a possession charge for the liquid-morphine, the one drug I didn't have a prescription for. I was released from the hospital the following morning, and pulled over again–just outside of the hotel I was about to check in to. They arrested me a second time, charging me with my second DUI in 6 hours.

My lawyer thought we had a good chance to fight both DUIs until I got the public intoxication charge a few weeks later for trying to make a phone call on my neighbor's slipper.

"Jason," my lawyer told me one day in court, "you need help."

Never something you want to hear from your attorney.

"Yeah, no shit," I countered. "That's why I hired you."

"No," he said, bluntly. "Like you need help."

"I don't need help," I countered. "I need the medication for my back."

"Jason," he said, "if you don't go get help, you're going to jail for a long time. They want to give you six months. If you do a few months in rehab, with time-served and half-time in California, you'll only have to do a few weeks inside."

I thought about his offer. With a body that still ached from the beatings in Mexican jail, further incarceration didn't sound too appealing. I'd do a little time in rehab, which would be better than jail, just to get the judge off my ass. But I DID NOT have a drug problem. I had a judge problem. I had a DA problem. If everyone could have just understood that I needed the drugs to wake up, to go to sleep, to go out, to come home, to eat, to breathe, to function, to not be sick — if they could only see this, then surely they'd drop the charges.

But they weren't going to see it my way. So I checked

myself into a rehab in Modesto, California in January 2009.

Rehab #1 was fairly uneventful. I went through my kick, which was softened by a methadone taper-down, and got the hell out. As far as I was concerned, I wasn't one of "them." These people were sucking dick for crank and banging their dealers to score. They were smoking crack and cooking dope in a spoon. Instead of focusing on our similarities—the need, the obsession, the dependence, the compulsive behavior, the utter disregard for others, the self-centered behavior, the self-destruction—I focused on the differences. *These* were drug addicts.

I wasn't a drug addict. I was just a guy who couldn't stop doing drugs.

Leaving rehab, I was smacked in the face by the realization that I was 29 years old and had no idea what I was going to do with my life. I couldn't go back to teaching high school because I was on probation for the next three years. I couldn't get a job doing anything, really, because I no longer had a drivers license.

Apparently, the state of California frowns upon getting multiple DUIs in a 24-hour period. I was deemed unfit for driving privileges for a year.

A month out of rehab, I was browsing online for jobs overseas. The problem, I decided once again, was my location. If I could just change that, things would be better. I would be better. Even though I wasn't using drugs anymore, they consumed my thoughts. I would wake up, dreaming about them. I needed them and I was pissed off that I wasn't allowed to take them.

Maybe if I moved far, far away, I could outrun the compulsion to use them. What I decided to do was what any rational trying-his-best-to-stay-clean-but-still-in-denial-he-has-a-real-problem drug addict would do: I took a job teaching English to children in Italy.

I applied for a position with Il Teatro Inglese (The English Theater). ITI was an Italian company that put on summer English camps for Italian middle school-aged children. I didn't read too much about the position. All I knew was it'd get me the fuck out of California and away from everyone's eyes anticipating my inevitable relapse.

When asked on the application if I'd ever been convicted of a crime, I lied, checking the "NO" box resoundingly. Shit, what was the worst that could happen? They find out and not hire me? I had nothing to lose.

I sent in my application and within a week I heard back. Apparently, Il Teatro Inglese forgot to do a background check. I was hired, instructed to arrive in Italy, by June 9.

But there was a problem—I was supposed to turn myself in to do a short jail sentence on June 5, 2009. The courts gave me time-served for the time I spent in rehab, but thanks to mandatory minimum sentences for DUIs, I had to do at least two weeks inside.

Hmm... jail or Italy?

We addicts have an innate ability to put shit off to deal with at a later time, perpetually irresponsible in a procrastinating fashion that would be impressive were it not so destructive. This is one of the difficulties of getting clean—the realization that you now have to deal with all of that shit you so easily brushed off before. What was once a small snowball is now a gigantic fucking avalanche of courtrooms and fines and jails and failures-to-appear, the realization that all of those people you fucked over and hurt in your addiction—you now have to face them, clean, sober, and look them in the eye to hear how much damage you caused in their lives.

It's overwhelming, and we only know three ways to deal with feeling overwhelmed: Run away, get high, or run away and get high.

I figured since my turn-in date was June 5th, I could leave on June 4th and not pop up on any screens through customs.

I was right.

I jumped bail and flew to Nice, France. From Nice I took a train across the Italian border and checked in to orientation for ITI. I expected a professional, academic environment with a small group of teachers.

What I found was a chaotic, alcohol-fueled, highly-sexualized world of youth and lust.

There were 120 teachers from all over the English-speaking world: Ireland, Scotland, England, South Africa, Australia, New Zealand, Canada, and the United States. We were all between 20 and 35 years old, and had an entire beach resort, on the Italian Riviera, rented out by ITI, at our disposal for a week.

The plan was for them to train us during a week-long orientation, before sending us in groups throughout Italy to teach at various camps.

The training was from 8:00 am to 4:30 pm. After that, we partied. I was roomed with two Irishmen and a Texan named Trevor. Every day, orientation would end and by 4:40 you could hear my Irish roommates clanking their way up the street, bags full of wine, yelling in what they claimed was English, though I still have my doubts, at Italian girls in bikinis who didn't understand anymore of what they were saying than I did.

We went hard. I'd never been a big drinker, but I

figured that as long as I wasn't doing drugs, I was ok. I maintained a steady .15 BAC for the duration of the week. Kids, youth, adventure, nothing-to-lose, living life in a foreign land and partying together before being shipped off like English-speaking cargo, to whatever town would allow us around their children.

On the day I should have turned myself in to jail in California, I was sitting alone on a beach in Italy, drinking a bottle of wine, when I was approached by a girl in a sundress.

"Hey, how's it goin'?" she asked, sitting down across from me.

She had cute, curly black hair a few inches past her chin, a thin frame, wearing a pair of red Ray Ban sunglasses that suited her personality and an attitude of extreme confidence that stopped just short of arrogance.

"I'm good," I said, the wine not yet bringing me the confidence I lacked while sober.

"Where you from?" she asked, smiling.

Every one of her mannerisms screamed "frisky." This girl sweated overt sexuality.

"California. And you?" I asked her, just as I noticed she wasn't wearing panties beneath her dress. This was not by accident.

She watched my eyes and just squinted. "Canada..."

For some reason I immediately thought of maple syrup and ice hockey.

"...and I was wondering..." she continued.

As she started to speak, she paused, stumbling not over what to say, but how to say it.

"... if it would be ok to ask youuuuu..." dragging out that last syllable, before stopping and blurting out, "to fuck me."

As the words left her lips, she had a look on her face like she'd just asked me to give her a cigarette or throw her a few bucks for gas. Slightly embarrassed, not for feeling what she felt, but for having to vocalize it. I found her wording curious. She didn't ask to fuck me, but rather for me to fuck her.

My chin dropped forward, and I just sat. Speechless.

"Is that too forward?" she asked, baiting me, eyebrows raised slightly.

This sure as shit beat jail.

"No, no..." was all I could get out. "Not at all."

"Look, you're fucking sexy, and I want you to fuck me," she said, looking me in my eyes. "If you don't want to, that's ok. But I just thought I'd ask."

Maple syrup and ice hockey. It was time I expanded my knowledge of our neighbors up north.

"Umm... yes, yes I can do that," I stuttered, trying to swig as much wine as I could before leaving the beach. "I can certainly do that."

Standing up and stumbling, the sand burning my feet, I followed her across the street and into the resort area.

Her room was downstairs, closest to the street and directly across from the swimming pool. She led me into her room where one of her roommates was doing her makeup on a neighboring bed, an attractive blonde, with a more athletic frame than the Canadian, fair-skinned with cute freckles.

"Don't mind her," said the Canadian.

"Hi, I'm Kelly," said the roommate, holding out her hand.

"She's from Scotland," the Canadian told me, as if I possibly could give a shit about geography at a time like this. "She's just going to watch." After a long pause, she asked, "Is that ok?"

Maple syrup and ice hockey. And haggis. I'll be goddamned.

"Do you guys have any wine?" I asked, both of them laughing at what was in reality a serious inquiry.

And just like that, I fulfilled the wish of a stranger from Canada, whose name I was never told, in front of a girl whose parents were probably at that precise moment bragging to their friends back in Scotland about how their daughter, Kelly, was off doing God's work teaching school children in Italy.

And that was just the second day.

The week went on like this. Sex, alcohol, more sex, followed by more alcohol. Condom and cheap Chianti sales were booming in the small Italian enclave that week, with people doing the types of things you only do when you're certain you'll never have to see the other person again. If the parents of the children we taught that summer had any idea where our mouths and hands and other parts had been during orientation, they would have yanked their kids from school and haz-matted up to give them a proper scrubbing.

It was a strange dichotomy. The morning after meeting the Canadian I watched her teach a group session on the value of Critical Pedagogy in the development of childhood consciousness. The day before I had her tied to a headboard with her roommate's scarf.

On my fourth day of orientation I was playing Frisbee with my Irish roommates when I fell into the swimming pool, drunk, and smacked my left ear against the water. It didn't hurt, but I couldn't hear out of it. No sound. At all.

The following day I asked one of the people in charge of the orientation about seeing a doctor for my ear.

"Ok," they told me, "the owner of the company, Brando, will be in later today. You can drive to the hospital with him."

Brando looked exactly like what you would picture someone named Brando to look like. He was a big, fat, hairy, old Italian man with mafia connects. In Italy you don't get the status of non-profit without having some inside connections, and Brando had them.

"Jay-zone?" he barked, breathing heavily from his walk up the slight incline from the parking lot.

"Si," I told him.

"Oh, parli Italiano?" he asked.

"Si."

His whole face lit up. For whatever reason, Brando really took a liking to me, slapping me on the shoulder. We drove to the hospital, sat in the waiting room together, and even saw the doctor together, demonstrating Brando's southern Italian complete disregard for personal space. After finding out that I had a small hole in my ear that may or may not heal on its own, Brando drove me back to the resort and dropped me off.

"Ciao Jay-zone!" he yelled, driving away. Brando looked ecstatic.

The following day, a lady who worked for ITI found me.

"Jason, you must go to the administrative office in town, right away," she told me, frantically. "It's an emergency."

I immediately thought I was fucked. I figured it either had something to do with my background check, my jumping bail, or my fucking strange Canadians. I was hoping it was the fucking of Canadians, but wasn't holding my breath.

As I approached the administrative office, I looked for cops. There were none that I could see, so I walked inside.

"Jason," the British receptionist told me, looking confused, "my name is Katyana." She gave me a fake 'nice to meet you' smile, but didn't hold her hand out. "I don't know what happened... or how this happened... but we've been advertising the position of Linguistics Director for months now, and Brando hasn't found anyone he likes." I stared at her, looking every bit as confused as she did. "Well," she continued, "...he wants to offer you the position."

Huh?

"You would teach the summer camps as planned," she said, "but when they're finished, you would start on a salaried position immediately. We'd pay for you to have a two-week vacation, after which you'd get a company car and drive around Italy to the different schools we are partnered with, assisting the local English teachers in their teaching curriculum."

Huh?

"You'd technically be a paid volunteer, meaning you don't need a work visa," she said, just as Brando walked into the room. "Or pay taxes."

"JAY-ZONE!" he belted out.

"Do you have a drivers license?" asked the receptionist.

"Umm... yes, of course," I told her. I pulled out my California ID card, which I had in place of the license the DMV had suspended. Brando put his hands out, having none of it.

"Basta," he told Katyana. He proceeded to tell her in Italian not to bother with formalities like drivers licenses, or documentation, or background checks. He demanded she just hire me.

And that's how a trying-his-best-to-stay-clean-but-still-in-denial-he-has-a-real-problem drug addict goes from jail in Tijuana to Rehab #1 to Linguistics Director of Il Teatro Inglese, in eight months time.

CHAPTER 8.

HOW TO SAY "I'M FUCKED" IN FRENCH

After the final camp was finished, I settled into the apartment that ITI was providing to enjoy my paid vacation. I made plans to spend the two weeks with an English girl named Kristina, a teacher from one of the camps that summer.

My relationship with Kristina was interesting. It wasn't romantic, but was at times sexual. Kristina was a fantastic teacher, someone whom the kids took to immediately and naturally. I was attracted less to her physical features – don't get me wrong, she was beautiful – and more to her excitement at teaching children and making a difference. At one point, I too possessed that excitement, that "fuck the odds, let's change the world" mentality. But the drug abuse destroyed that thing inside of me, whatever it was. Even clean, I couldn't seem to get it back.

Our plan was to hole-up in my small apartment and just enjoy the ocean for a few weeks. After a few days, Kristina started growing restless and wanted to take a day-trip to Nice, France. A change of scenery for a day sounded harmless so I agreed to tag along.

In Europe, they charge you to use the beaches. Beaches

are divided by different colored umbrellas and beach chairs, each equally overpriced and overcrowded with typical European flair. Of course, there is always the "free beach," usually a sliver of rocks and insects, tucked underneath a cliff, sitting between the for-pay beaches. But Kristina hated the free beach, meaning I was going to pay to occupy a section of sand. Just as we sat down, Kristina started writhing in pain, holding her head.

"Jason," she said. "I think I'm getting a migraine."

"Ok... what do you want to do?" I replied.

"Can we go see if I can get something from the Pharmacy?"

At this point, I avoided pharmacies. I didn't even like walking by them. Inside I could actually smell the pills, that powder-like scent that triggered something from inside me that I wanted to forget. That I came to Europe to outrun. If I just pretended that I left that monster behind in California, then maybe—just maybe—it would go away.

"You can go," I said in a way that sounded much more dick-ish than I intended. "I think I'll stay here."

This would have been a superb time to confess to Kristina my past, but confession meant recollection, and recollection meant acknowledgement, and that wasn't going to happen.

"For fuck's sake, Jason, can you come with me? I can barely see." She pushed her hand against her left eye, obviously in extreme pain.

"Yeah... I can come."

We walked into the first building with a green cross outside that we could find, a small pharmacy tucked behind a cafe and a store that smelled of overpriced sunscreen and beach towels.

The moment we walked in, it hit me. That smell. God, that smell.

"Bonjour, umm... medicine?" as I pointed to Kristina whose migraine was intensifying by the second. "Migraine," I said, hoping the word in French was similar to English.

"Oui, oui," said the pharmacist. Reaching behind the counter she pulled out a blue box and handed it to Kristina. "This for her," said the pharmacist, pointing to Kristina.

This was my gig. I'd been to so many pharmacies, in so many countries, scoring drugs in bulk as I schemed and scammed my way to getting well. There was something about the ritual that gripped me. This ritual of asking the pharmacist, disregarding whatever half-hearted warning they offered, walking outside and popping or snorting. The ritual—just this simple act of getting a box from a pharmacist—it awoke something inside of me. And no matter how hard I tried to ignore it, its presence was constant.

Kristina took two of the tablets and asked if we could just go back to my apartment so she could lie down. After about 15 minutes, the pain in her head was gone.

"Jason, are you ok?" asked Kristina as we walked toward the train station. "You sure got quiet."

My insides were turning. My natural state was the one I felt inside of that pharmacy. Among the drugs, I felt at peace. Asking for and getting drugs, even over the counter ones, made me feel normal, which only made me realize how abnormal I'd been feeling for the previous eight months. Something was wrong with me. I was a psychological mess, which was far more than I was willing to divulge to Kristina.

"Yeah, I'm good," I told her while I stared at the ground. We boarded the train to return to my apartment in Italy, and Kristina was acting noticeably different. She became flirty and romantic, which was outside of the scope of our relationship. She was experiencing some sort of chemically-induced euphoria, something I recognized immediately. I knew that feeling. I could sense it. I longed for it.

As the French countryside passed us on the left, the Mediterranean to our right, Kristina started to nod out.

I looked on in admiration. Fuck, I missed that feeling. But how...?

"It was over the counter," I told myself. "It's nothing more than aspirin, Jason. Relax."

Suddenly, Kristina shot up and ran to the bathroom. She returned ten minutes later, sweating.

"That medicine made me throw up," she said, looking high, eyelids getting lazy.

Opiates often make someone without a tolerance vomit. The pieces to a sadistic, diabolical puzzle were falling into place, and it excited me. My mouth was starting to water, a Pavlovian response from my classically conditioned brain that hadn't tasted opiates in far too long.

Sitting back down, Kristina leaned up against the train window and fell asleep, nodding out into an oblivion that looked all-too-familiar and oh-so-appealing.

As Kristina slept, I decided on a little light reading. Picking up the blue pill box, I did my best to understand just what exactly was in these tablets. Everything was in French, but I could make out one thing:

Codeine.

Sometimes, as a drug addict, the drugs find you.

Mexico, jail, Mexican jail, courts, lawyers, fines, DMV, a career that I threw away–they all flashed before my eyes as we crossed the French-Italian border.

But those things were back home. I bet, if I try really hard, I can take the drugs responsibly in Italy. The problem wasn't me. Isn't me. I can do this.

With Kristina knocked out, leaning against the train window, I took four tablets out of the box and stared at them. *"Fuck, I missed you."* It was like picking up the love of my life–my soulmate–from the airport after an eight month absence. Reaching into Kristina's backpack, I pulled out a bottle of water and sat it between my legs. I chewed up the pills so they'd hit harder and washed them down.

And I waited.

It only took about ten minutes. Suddenly, I simultaneously felt defeat and success, realizing that I'd just thrown away 32 weeks of clean time. Jail, rehab, withdrawal, detox, everything I went through—for nothing. At the same time, my insides tumbled, heated up and elevated, my limbs tingling. My everything.

I grabbed the box. Since I already threw away my clean time, I figured, *"Fuck it. If you're gonna do it Jason, then DO IT."*

The box came with 20 tablets, meaning 14 pills remained. I took all 14 and threw the box away in the train bathroom, three cars down. This is an old drug addict trick. When you steal someone's medication, you never just take a handful. People notice when their shit's half gone. That's a rookie mistake. What you do is take the whole thing and let them think they somehow misplaced it while establishing plausible deniability. "You can't find your bottle? Here, I'll happily spend the next hour helping you find the drugs I just stole." You've already dumped the pills into the side of your shoe, placing the empty bottle in your other shoe. You can't chance them hearing the rattling sound they'd make in the bottle. They eyeball your pockets, seeing nothing, but you're safe regardless because you didn't put them in your pockets.

You're in the clear.

It's interesting how quickly I went from, "I'll take the drugs responsibly here in Italy" to "Fuck it, if I'm going to go out, I'm going to go out with a bang." It took about ten minutes, the same amount of time it took the drugs to hit my system. All sense of reason goes out the window, and "active-addiction" picks up where it left off. They call addiction a progressive disease, meaning you don't ever get to start over. Whatever miserable, fucked up state of existence forced you to get clean last time — that's where you pick up. That's your starting point.

The misery leaves the light on for you.

Kristina spent the following week with me, which kept getting interrupted by my quick trips to Menton, the first French town past the border. In France you could buy codeine over the counter; in Italy you could not. My life suddenly consisted of frequent trips to Menton, where I'd spend my entire paycheck on train tickets and pills, purchasing 15–20 boxes at a time. I had this idea that if I just bought two boxes from 10 pharmacies, it was somehow not as bad as if I bought 20 boxes from a single pharmacy. Like the alcoholic who buys 10 airplane-sized bottles of vodka, hoping nobody will notice.

I was able to function. Once I re-established my tolerance, which didn't take long, I was able to work without anybody noticing. I drove the company car all throughout Italy, north of Rome to various schools to assist their English teachers in developing curriculum. My typical routine consisted of popping about 12 codeine pills, working, smiling, laughing, and feeling good. I felt alive again. My rapport with the schools and teachers got rave reviews, and Brando was extremely satisfied with my performance.

"See?" I'd think while I drove, window down, high, through the Italian night to my next school. *"I can do it! I can do both! I can do drugs AND have a normal life!"*

That all changed when I met Liana, a teacher from Bergamo, just outside of Milan. Liana had a heart of pure gold, the exact type we drug addicts seek out to manipulate and drain of any and all services.

On my second night in Bergamo, Liana invited me to drinks with her friend Marcello. The three of us sat outside of a beautiful cafe, up on a hill, looking down at the city of Milan.

After introductions, I discovered Marcello was a psychiatrist. Careful not to pounce too quickly, I waited until the time was right.

"In America, psychiatrists can write prescriptions. Is it the same here?" I asked, prying.

"Yes, yes, of course. It's the same," said Marcello.

"I have a psychiatrist in California," I lied. "He's really good."

Marcello looked on, not realizing the magic trick I was about to pull off.

"Do you mind if I ask why you see a psychiatrist in California?" asked Liana, falling into my trap.

Marcello snapped at her in Italian, admonishing her for asking such a personal question.

"No, no, it's ok," I assured Marcello, acting just

embarrassed enough to drum up the precise amount of sympathy I'd need for this to work. "He's actually a friend of mine. I don't have health insurance, so he helps prescribe me medication for my headaches."

"Headaches?" they both asked, confused.

"Yes, I get really bad migraines. He prescribes me Xanax—Alprazolam, I believe is the name of it in Italy," I said, pretending as if I didn't already know how to say Xanax in 5 different languages. "For some reason they get really bad in the autumn," I told them, autumn just a week away. "They're seasonal."

Liana looked at Marcello. "Marcello, can't you help him?"

"Umm... yes, I can do that, I suppose," he said, hesitantly, clearly not appreciating being put on the spot like that.

"Oh, can you?" I said to Marcello, doing my best to act surprised. "Wow, I never would have thought about asking you. Thank you so much."

Eight months clean be damned, my powers of manipulation were in tact. I didn't ask him for the pills. I got him to offer them to me.

I waited to take the Xanax from Marcello until I got back. I was due for a week off and my plan consisted of getting as high as possible and disappearing. I drove straight through the night, excited and anxious. Pulling up to my apartment, I parked my car, burst into the bedroom, threw my bags down with anticipation and immediately downed four of the 1-mg Xanax and 12 of the codeine pills with a Lipton Iced Tea, and let it all set in.

Just as the high punched me square in the chest, I heard a pounding on my door.

KNOCK-KNOCK-KNOCK

I couldn't focus my eyes, and as soon as I stood up I fell right back down, smacking my eye on the nightstand and cutting my forehead. As I forced my way to the door, I could feel blood trickling down my cheek. I opened the door and saw Brando standing there with a frantic look on his face.

"Jay-zone," he said between heavy breaths, "we have a problem. You have to go to London."

"London, what? It's my week off."

"What happened to your head?" he asked, concerned. "And your shirt?"

I looked down and saw a burn in my shirt from nodding out with a lit cigarette in my hand.

"Oh, I was drinking," I assured him, choosing the one drug where it'd be socially acceptable to nod off with a cigarette in your hand. "It's nothing."

Brando proceeded to tell me that the law was changing in Italy and now even paid volunteers needed a work visa. The thing with Brando and ITI was they were always operating on the fringes of legality. It was a racket that made Brando a shit-ton of money. We didn't pay the teachers — they were volunteers who were housed with families. And the camps weren't cheap, with parents spending close to 1,000 Euros to send a kid for the summer.

Brando in a nutshell: He had a yacht in Croatia that was bought through the company. Once a year he'd take a crippled kid onto the yacht for a few hours, take pictures to document it, and use it as a tax write-off. He'd then send the crippled kid home, just as his mistress arrived.

"Ok, fuck, Brando, when do I have to go?" I asked.

"Now."

The story didn't add up. It wouldn't have added up had I been sober. But Brando had the connections and knew the types of people where you didn't ask too many questions. If Brando needed me in London, I was going to London, like it or not.

"When you get to London, call me, and I'll tell you what to do," he told me.

Reaching into his pocket, I assumed he was going to give me a plane ticket. Instead, he handed me cash, 2000 Euros. I'd never seen a 500 Euro note until he handed me four of them.

"Buy your ticket from Nice to London, leaving tonight. And Jay-zone—CALL ME WHEN YOU GET TO LONDON."

The high from the Xanax was progressing rapidly, so I figured it was best not to argue. Grabbing my luggage, iced tea and passport, I got into Brando's car and tried to gather my senses.

Brando asked me over and over on the car ride if I was ok. "Jason," he'd beg me, "What's wrong with you? You look like a different person."

"I'm just tired, Brando," I said. "You got me driving all over Italy. That shit's tiring."

Brando dropped me at the train station, where I boarded a train for Nice, nodding in and out of consciousness as I walked. Once aboard safely, I took four more Xanax, and another eight codeine. By the time I arrived at the airport, I was in full on blackout mode.

Approaching the airport counter, I put one of the 500 Euro notes on the counter and demanded a ticket to London.

"I need a ticket to London," flashing the lady a sarcastic

smile, the Xanax doing its best to turn me into a total asshole.

She said something in rapid French, and I looked at her, amused.

"No French. Sorry."

She raised her voice, and I started yelling at her in Italian. "Just give me a fucking ticket to London!"

A police officer came over and put his hand on my arm.

"Get the fuck off me," I said in English, yanking my arm away.

"Sir," the officer told me, "you must go."

"Fuck you, man, I need a ticket to London," I demanded.

This officer glared at me, embarrassed by the scene I was creating. "This is for rental car."

I looked up and realized I wasn't at the ticket counter. I wasn't even close to the ticket counter. A gigantic sign that read "EUROPCAR" looked down at me, while a crowd of people gathered around.

"Oh…"

I picked up my bags and stumbled in the direction of the real ticket counter. The officer followed me, putting his hand on my shoulder, gently, genuinely concerned. "Sir, are you ok?"

"Fuck you, man, get your hand off me."

Like I said, total asshole.

The next available flight to London left at 9:30 p.m., landing in London at 10:30 p.m. I didn't yet know where I was going to sleep once I got there, and I was in no condition to be roaming the streets of London, so I bought a ticket for the following morning, 8:50 a.m.

Diving into the back seat of the first taxi I could find, I instructed the driver to take me to the city center.

"You don't have luggage?" he asked.

"No."

I left all of my bags, all of my belongings, right there on the airport curb. I don't know why, but I had a history of doing things like this on Xanax. I can't really explain it. I'd wake up from blackouts with no wallet, no phone, nothing. Xanax put in me a total "fuck it" state of mind.

I woke up to the cab driver hitting me in the arm, telling me to get out of his cab. I paid him and began roaming the streets of Nice, high out of my mind. Passing a sign that advertised medical services, I got the bright idea to score some stronger narcotics. Codeine was ok, but I had a hunch France had more to offer a drug addict like me, wallet bursting open with my boss's money.

To this day, I have no idea how I found a doctor who was willing to prescribe me opiates, given the shape I was in. Sure, I was good at manipulating doctors, but I couldn't even hold my head up. It was too heavy. Slumped against the doorway, I rang the bell and waited. Finally, I was welcomed in by what I remember to be an attractive older woman, though I was so gone, who knows. I gave her some story about migraines, and she asked me point-blank what I wanted.

When you're trying to score from a doctor you're not familiar with, it's like going to the swap meet. You start high, with a request like OxyContin. The doctor then counters with a drug like Ibuprofen. Eventually, you meet in the middle with a drug like Percocet.

"Do they have OxyContin in France?" I asked. Oxy was never my drug of choice. I was just using it to start the bargaining process.

"Yes, but that is very strong," she said. "Only one pharmacy in Nice carries it."

"Well…" I began, annoyed, "do you know which one it is?"

"Yes," she said, "it's my sister's pharmacy. I call to see if she is open."

She disappeared and I nodded out in the chair, too high to really appreciate what ridiculously dumb luck I was experiencing.

"Yes," I heard her say, before I could see her. "Yes, she open. But you must go now. They close at 4:30."

She handed me a prescription and a map, which I didn't even bother trying to follow. I interrupted total strangers, pointed to the map, and they'd point me in the right direction. Stranger after stranger pointed me in the right direction until I finally arrived. The sister was there, waiting for me.

"This is very expensive," she warned. "450 Euro for one box." I had a feeling I was getting ripped off by this lady and her sister, but I didn't care. It wasn't my money.

Without hesitation I put down a 500 Euro note, grabbed the box, and walked off without collecting my change.

"Merci," I muttered, not loud enough for anyone to hear. "Merci."

I walked to the nearest hotel and checked in, sans abandoned luggage–which for all I knew was setting off terror alerts back at the airport. Almost half of the money Brando had given me was gone, and I hadn't even left the airport.

Sitting on the edge of the hotel bed, I pulled the dresser out and looked at my pills: 80-mg OxyContin tablets, 20 of them. I wasn't as familiar with Oxy as I was with other drugs, but at this point, I was beyond rational thought anyway. I swallowed four of the tablets with the iced tea–the one thing I'd managed to not lose on this journey. Using the handle of the telephone, I crushed the OxyContin tablet into a powder, rolled up one of the 500 Euro notes, and snorted about a quarter of it.

Walking outside, people were staring at me. Hard. As I walked, they'd cross the street, making sure to keep to the other side like I was some kind of narcotic leper. People stopped, letting me pass, all looking half-concerned, half-entertained.

I tried to light a cigarette but was unable to hold it. It kept falling out of my hand, onto the street. As I bent over to pick up the cigarette that I no longer had the dexterity to hold, I sliced my head against the bottom of a stop sign, cutting the left side of my forehead. I felt blood gushing, dripping down my chin and onto my shirt, yet I didn't care. I couldn't have possibly given less of a fuck about the world at that point.

Fuck the world.

I tried it their way. The world said I had to stop doing drugs, and I stopped. And was miserable. I'd watch people in restaurants smiling, joking, laughing, and wonder how they were so fucking happy if THIS is what it felt like to be clean and sober. How could they be so happy and not be high? It was all bullshit, some inside joke that everybody was in on but me. For eight months I stopped getting high, and I hated myself. My demons, my hurt, the pain, they just sat there, un-medicated, screaming my name at night.

It was time to try it my way.

Again.

With cuts now on both sides of my forehead, I was losing a fairly significant amount of blood. I found a nice, quaint little cafe, nestled snuggly along the beautiful beaches of the French Riviera, and sat down. This was the kind of place where couples come, a few hundred feet from the beach, romantic and charming with lit candles and red wine. And in walks this American, t-shirt and flip flops, high on OxyContin, Xanax, and codeine, bleeding from his forehead, stumbling through tables and chairs, like Godzilla on drugs.

"You go now!" screamed the owner.

"Fuuuuuuck you," was all I could muster, in a sarcastic, nonchalant tone that is more likely than not the real reason the French hate us.

Hiccup

I sat down, leaning back in a chair, while the cafe owner was about to have a heart attack.

"You go!" he screamed at me. "You go!"

Hiccup *Hiccup*

They were coming faster now, and I knew this was a problem.

Hiccup *Hiccup* *Hiccup*

When people die of an opiate overdose, they die of respiratory failure. Your body actually relaxes to the point of forgetting to breathe, shutting down completely. Hiccups were my body's first stage of an overdose, a last-ditch attempt at getting some oxygen. I'd gotten the hiccups before when using, and would immediately find a cold shower to wake me up, shocking the body back into compliance. But I was nowhere near a shower and much too high to try and find one.

Hiccup *Hiccup* *Hiccup* *Hiccup*

I was dying and I knew it.

Hiccup *Hiccup* *Hiccup* *Hiccup*

And I didn't care.

Hiccup *Hiccup* *Hiccup* *Hiccup*

That's how good it felt.

Hiccup *Hiccup* *Hiccup* *Hiccup*

If I'd known dying felt this good, I might have tried harder earlier on.

After my last hiccup, I closed my eyes and fell over sideways in my chair, bringing the table with me. All of a sudden—the taste. It's unmistakable. That yellow shit from giving Mark mouth-to-mouth. That taste—I tasted it.

That bitter taste of dying.

I heard the chair crash to the ground, felt the cold ground against my cheek, and went to sleep peacefully, while the cafe owner, the tourists, and the Gypsy playing an accordion for tips looked on in stunned silence.

I jumped out of my skin with force. The doctor shot me up with Naloxone, immediately countering the effects of the drugs. Naloxone blocks your opiate receptors, throwing you into immediate withdrawal. Looking up, I could see one doctor and six French police officers.

"Where did you buy the OxyContin?" asked one of the officers. The doctor just looked on, with an expression of disgust.

It looked like we were in a parking garage. The room was oval, with blinding lights and concrete everywhere.

"What?" I asked, playing dumb.

The officer held up the box of OxyContin. "Where did you buy this?"

"Those aren't mine, man."

Honesty and active-addiction don't mesh well. To maintain a respectable level of narcotic-tainted blood, a solid, sturdy foundation of total bullshit and asinine stories is essential. We addicts will come up with tales that are so out there, so gone, so off-the-wall-fucking unfathomable, that the lie's maintenance requires a whole other set of ridiculous fibs, lies, and half-truths. It's layer-upon-layer of bullshit, to the point where we forget what is true and what is not. There are lies that, in active addiction, I could've told and passed a polygraph, displaying neither fear of detection (What? Detect what? Those aren't mine!) nor cognitive dissonance (That's my story and I'm sticking to it). This is sociopathic behavior, and make no mistake about it—to maintain a drug addiction and do the things we do to those who love us most without thinking twice is the very definition of a sociopath.

"Nah, dude," I said, looking at the officer and suddenly speaking fluent Californian. "There must be a mistake."

The officer doing all of the talking stared me down. "Ok," he said, before turning around and walking off while the other officers followed close behind.

"Hey, you can't take that," I begged.

"Take what?" he asked in fluent English. "This isn't yours, remember?"

The police walked off with my OxyContin and the doctor had me discharged, leaving me nowhere to go. Making matters worse, I pulled a typical Xanax-blackout move and lost my wallet and cell phone. The entire 2000 Euros Brando had given me was now gone.

I went to hail a taxi, but realized I had no money. I walked for over an hour, the promise of the Xanax in my room the only thing that kept me going through the agony of withdrawal.

"Hello, I think I lost my room key," I said to the man working the desk.

"Your name?" he asked.

"Jason Smith."

"I see here," he explained, "you check out Sunday morning."

"Sunday morning? Wait...fuck, what day is it?"

"It is Tuesday, sir," he told me, which was absolutely no help.

"What about my stuff? My passport? There was some medicine?"

"No, we don't have anything," he said.

"What? I had a passport and some Xanax!" I yelled.

"Sir, there was nothing in your room."

Just then I vaguely remembered at some point in my blackout returning to my room for my passport and more Xanax. But it felt like a dream. I realized I could no longer distinguish between fantasy and reality. I didn't know what was real anymore.

"Is it night time?"

"Yes, sir. It's night time," he said, starting to look concerned.

Walking out of the hotel, I walked until I found the train station, where the homeless were sleeping. I curled up under one of the benches and closed my eyes. Just as I was finally drifting off to sleep, a police officer nudged me with his boot to tell me that it was midnight, and I had to leave the station and sleep outside. Making matters worse, it started to rain.

Finding a bush that offered slight cover from the rain, I curled up into a ball and thought about my life.

This right here should have been my "bottom." You often hear addicts talk about hitting rock bottom and having a moment of clarity, where they see the destruction they're causing in the world and decide to make a personal change. This entire fiasco came less than a week from my meeting Marcello, the psychiatrist who prescribed me the Xanax. I had no luggage, no wallet, no cell phone, no passport, no money, and was fairly certain I had no more job, because how the fuck do you explain losing 2,000 Euros to your boss when you didn't even make it out of the airport? This should have been my bottom. I wish I could say it was.

I slept outside the Nice train station for three nights, in the pouring rain, when one of my homeless counterparts recommend I go to the American Consular agency. It wasn't an embassy, or a consulate, but they provided services to Americans who'd been struck by hardship while traveling. I had taken to stealing bread off of café tables and drinking out of public bathroom sinks. As if my situation weren't depressing enough, the come-down from the Xanax was psychologically paralyzing, gripping me with a level of despair and depression I'd never felt before. Plus, I was physically sick from the codeine/Oxy kick.

It was dark.

I got to the Consular Agency three hours before it opened because there really isn't shit else to do when you wake up to a rain-drenched sunrise. I had my story all planned out: I got robbed, they took everything, I had nothing, poor me, please help, blah, blah, blah.

The lady at the Consular Agency explained how everything worked. They would help me get a hotel room and contact my family back home. The woman working that day called around and found me a hotel room at a discounted rate. We tried calling my family, but they weren't taking my calls. You know it's bad when you're homeless in a foreign country and your family doesn't want anything to do with you. But could you blame them?

It's human nature to eventually cut ties with someone who's causing you the amount of emotional pain I was causing them.

The lady at the Consular finally got through to my mom on the phone. "Hello, my name is Sylvia, I'm with the American Consular Services in Nice, France. Your son, Jason, has been robbed and needs help. I…"

My mom cut her off, and I could see Sylvia's face go blank.

"She wants to talk to you," Sylvia told me, hesitantly handing me the phone.

Taking the phone, I began to give my mom a sob story. "Mom," I said, "some guys robbed me and…"

She cut me off.

"Jason, I'm going to say this one time. I can't do this anymore," she said, holding back tears. "I hate to do this…" As she took a deep breath, I knew whatever was coming next wasn't going to be pretty.

"You are dead to me."

And she hung up the phone.

There exists no bond stronger than the one between a mother and her child, and my addiction had taken my mom to places where her only way of coping was to pretend I was dead. Death, while difficult, at least leads to a place of closure, and real or not, it would allow her to move on with her life. I couldn't really blame her.

"Jason," said Sylvia, snapping me out of the reality of my own mother writing me off as dead, "we can give you 50 Euro to get a train ticket to the consulate in either Paris or Florence. The hotel is paid for. I wish you luck."

Sylvia was on to me. But at least she would give me a little money to eat, get some water, and a train ticket. My plan was to buy a train ticket to Florence, because at least there I could speak the language and I was familiar with the surroundings. I thanked Sylvia and reached into my back pocket where my wallet should have been before remembering the tragic reality in which I was living, one with no identification, phone, or family.

Placing the money into my pocket, I felt a piece of paper. Pulling it out, I could see that I still had a prescription for Xanax and OxyContin that the pharmacy never collected from me. The prescription was good for two fills, and I had a single stamp on the paper indicating that I'd already had one fill.

This meant I had one fill of each–Xanax and OxyContin–remaining.

If you want to really understand the desperation and depravity of drug addiction, here you go. I wanted to stop with every fiber of my being, but could not. Nothing obliterates the human spirit and self- esteem more than using a substance against your own will, buying and putting in while hating every second of it. I was homeless, living outside of a train station, in Nice, France. I was stealing bread and drinking from public toilets. And when given money to survive–to eat, to re-hydrate, to live like a civilized primate–I chose the drugs.

An old man named Arthur once told me about a study where they got a monkey hooked on heroin. They hooked the monkey to the point where he was consistently choosing heroin over food and water. They then forced him to kick, keeping him from the drug for a few weeks. After the monkey went through his withdrawal and began eating and drinking with regularity, they offered him the choice of heroin again. The monkey flipped the fuck out, throwing a tantrum and destroying his cage to get away from the drug. He wanted no part of the heroin, having lived through the treachery and physical dependence of the drug.

I wanted so badly to be like that monkey.

I didn't have enough money to buy the Oxy, so I loaded up on Xanax and spent a few days passed out on the beach. I was so high that I never stopped to think what I must have looked like. My forehead had two giant scabs on it, and I'd fallen down so many times that my arms and face were completely bruised over. I was sunburnt from passing out in the sun, exacerbating the dehydration from not drinking much water.

Once the drugs were out, I stowed my way in a train bathroom for the entire trip from Nice to Milan, and then again from Milan to Florence. I locked the train bathroom and sat there for hours, avoiding the guy checking tickets and trying to cry quietly enough to not be heard.

When I finally arrived in Florence, I walked to the US Consulate and told them my story about getting robbed. I was about to take out a loan from the US State Department when they got through to my sister, who agreed to pay for my ticket home. My dad reluctantly agreed to pick me up from the airport.

I cried the entire way home, but not heavy sobs. Light, Xanax-withdrawal whimpers, pathetic and soft. Landing in San Francisco, I didn't even have any luggage to collect.

"Jas," my dad told me upon seeing me, "you look like you're dying."

"How'd that feel," my sponsor asked.

"How'd what feel?"

"Hearing your dad say that you looked like you were dying."

I thought for a minute, before realizing the answer was somewhat terrifying.

"It didn't."

Truth is, I didn't feel it. I didn't feel anything. They use opiates to mask pain, but they're not smart-bombs. They're carpet-bombs and they annihilate anything in their path. They're not able to pinpoint which pain to hit, and which to ignore. They just numb all of it, and when you do drugs as long as I did drugs, there comes a point where there's nothing left. I couldn't feel. My dad wasn't the first person to tell me I looked like I was dying. I'd lied to and manipulated and stole from anybody who was close to me, and there's a reason for that: They were easy targets. The ones who love us the most tend to be the ones who are closest to us, and their proximity makes them obvious marks. Harming them doesn't feel good, nor does it feel bad – it simply doesn't feel like anything.

Our family members often ask us things like, "How could you do this to me?" or tell us things like, "But you made me a promise." What they don't understand is NONE OF IT MATTERS. You're trying to incorporate human emotion into inhumane and emotionless behavior. You're projecting your own ability to feel guilt, shame, remorse onto the actions of someone who feels none of these things. It's like trying to make a dog feel guilty for taking food off the counter – they don't understand that you just worked hard preparing that meal. They were acting on pure Freudian id, fulfilling a need at their core. Your feelings never came into the equation. No offense–it's nothing personal. It's strictly business.

Until, of course, we get clean. Then – believe me – we feel that shit and it's heavy.

"So Europe was a bust?" my sponsor asked, mockingly. "It didn't cure you?"

"Nope."

"What'd you do?" he asked.

"I went to China," I said rapidly, as if I was trying to just get that absurd decision out into the open and out of the way.

"...I went to China."

CHAPTER 9.

THE LAWYERS MADE ME CHANGE THIS CHAPTER TITLE

I'm pretty sure The Leviathan doesn't really do background checks. I just want to get that out of the way for future reference.

I call it The Leviathan because they're of such mighty, intimidating stature that the legal team of this publisher found it necessary to wipe any and all references that might lead one to decipher their identity from this book. That's power.

As I was saying, I'm fairly certain The Leviathan doesn't really do background checks.

Returning home from France, nobody wanted me around. My mom had essentially disowned me, my sister was busy telling everyone "I told you so" regarding my addiction, and my friends were all now married with children.

At some point, while I was off getting high, life happened for everyone else. My friends acquired actual lives, lives that were so far beyond anything I could hope to acquire. Family. Wives. Children. Careers. Real lives that took years to obtain – lives that didn't come via the instant gratification to which I'd grown accustomed, and therefore lives that were beyond anything I could ever hope for.

When I got home, I was promptly arrested and extradited to the San Luis Obispo jail to serve the sentence I skipped out on when I jumped bail and flew to Nice. They made me serve the entire sentence, plus an additional 50% for fleeing the country. Upon my release, my father picked me up. The walk from the jail to my dad's truck was just as shameful as the walk to his truck from the airport after the fiasco in France.

They didn't raise me this way, which would have hurt had I been able to feel.

With nowhere to go, I stayed at his house. My father was nothing but supportive, encouraging me to go to meetings and to get out of bed. I think deep down he felt guilty for what happened with my uncle Mark. I tried going to a few AA meetings but I hated it. A bunch of people sitting around, bitching about their problems – at least, that's what I chose to see. They were alcoholics, and I hated alcohol. They had problems, I didn't. All of my problems stemmed from things other people had done to me. Doctors who prescribed to me, friends and family who abandoned me, jobs that fired me, law enforcement who picked on me. If everybody would just leave me the fuck alone, I'd be all right.

When everyone finally left me alone, I became bitter toward them for leaving me, maintaining my pathetic, perpetual victimization.

Anyway, like I was saying–I'm fairly certain The Leviathan doesn't really do background checks. I was alone and angry, wanting to jump out of my own skin, looking at various jobs overseas when I came across a posting for an English teaching job in China. The thought of working for any company in my current state – let alone a company like The Leviathan-made me chuckle. I applied, almost as a gag, once again with the "what's the worst that can happen?" mentality. I was 30 years old, living at my dad's house, no job, no driver's license, no car. I was fresh out of jail, on probation for drug charges, two DUI charges, and jumping bail internationally, when I got the call from someone named Nick with The Leviathan.

I think a corporation like The Leviathan banks on the belief that nobody with a criminal record would be qualified enough to get a job that high up in the company, or if they were, they wouldn't have the balls to apply.

They would be wrong.

"Jason," he told me over the phone, "we've received your resume and are very interested. Do you have a minute?"

Nick proceeded to interview me while I proceeded to tell him what he wanted to hear.

"Ok, Jason, I'm going to present your resume to my boss, and I'll let you know by the end of the week if you've been hired."

"Ok," was all I could muster, incredulous at the prospect.

"Oh, Jason, one more thing – your background check. Is there anything that might show up?"

"Nope."

"Ok, because at The Leviathan, we obviously do very thorough background checks. There's nothing that might be alarming?"

You mean other than the fact that I just got out of jail and am on probation for the next 3 years?

"Nope."

"Ok, Jason, I'll be in contact soon."

Nick called two days later to offer me the position of English Language Director at one of The Leviathan's schools in China.

The stench of my cell still fresh, I was hired by The Leviathan to oversee an entire language school, along with a staff of twenty teachers, and close to a hundred small children. They even paid for my flight.

True story.

I met Elise between my time in jail and leaving for China. In the beginning, Elise was a healthy enabler. I had no access to any drugs while at my dad's house – my family informed the doctors I'd been scamming, so they weren't an option. The pill game on the street was much too expensive for my blood. When I first started using in 1997, you could buy Norcos on the street for about 25 cents apiece. By 2010, they cost $4.00 apiece. As of 2014, they go for $6.00 apiece. If the rule of supply and demand is to be believed, America has a prescription drug problem that is flourishing on the streets, projecting skyward.

But I digress.

Elise worked taking care of an elderly lady with Alzheimer's, and I talked her into bringing me some of the lady's pain meds here and there. Nothing extreme, just a Vicodin here, a Valium there. Elise had never seen the passed-out-in-the-train-station Jason, or the kicking-Fentanyl-in-a-Tijuana-jail-cell Jason. I kept that guy hidden and much like my interview with The Leviathan, showed her the guy I knew she wanted to see.

Elise has a big heart, and those are the easiest to take advantage of.

ME: "Man, my back is really hurting. Did I tell you there's a titanium cage in my spine? It is killing me."

ELISE: "Oh, you poor thing! Can't you take anything for it?"

ME: "I could, but I don't have health insurance. It fucking sucks. I can't sleep at night, I can't stand up straight. I don't know what to do."

ELISE: "Oh, I am so sorry! Is there anything I can do to help?"

ME: "No, I guess I'll just have to suffer."

ELISE: "Wait, the lady I take care of has pain meds that most of the time she doesn't even take. Maybe I can bring you those, if that'll help?"

ME: "Oh my god, that'd be a life saver! Thank you so much!"

Once again, I didn't ask. I got her to offer, like it was her idea. A proper drug addict, through-and-through.

It's too easy to take advantage of the people in this world who deserve far better than what someone like me has to offer.

Elise and I dated for the few months leading up to my departure for China. We got along well, but I couldn't fall in love with her. I couldn't fall in love with anybody – drugs had my heart and weren't about to loosen their grip.

In active addiction, I can't love you. I just can't, so don't even try. I know I won't. I had the most incredible girlfriends through the years, amazing girls who truly loved me, unconditionally, through my addiction and the sleazy shit I did to maintain it. I never dated another addict. Never. I always had girlfriends who were "normal," most of whom didn't even drink. They loved me wholeheartedly, and in return I let them be my mistress.

That's the God's honest truth. If I'm in active addiction, I am incapable of intimacy. I have a thing with the drugs, and we're big on fidelity. We're madly in love, a passionate, sensual relationship. They're the last things I think of before I go to sleep (do I have enough to not be sick in the morning?), they're the first things I think of when I wake up (what time will my dealer wake up?). All day I think about them (if I could just get more, I'll be ok) and when I work, I work for them (how much money did I make today, and how much can I buy with it?).

I spend all day fantasizing about how good they're going to make me feel when I see them next.

Any girl who came along was my mistress; they just didn't know it. This might also explain why every girlfriend I've ever had thought I was cheating on them. They were certain of it. The behaviors for maintaining a drug addiction are the same as someone who is unfaithful. The lying, being sneaky, coming home late, money going missing, acting funny, unexplainable behavior. Plus, opiates obliterate your sex drive, leaving your girlfriend to assume you must be getting it from somewhere else.

You can perform on opiates. You just don't feel like it.

"I'm going grocery shopping," I'd say, at 6 a.m. on a Saturday morning because when you're a drug addict, you live according to your dealer's schedule and availability. I'd be gone for three hours, come home with no money and a fucking bag of Doritos from the gas station, ready to concoct one of my asinine, ludicrous, ridiculous stories that would make sense of this insanity, arguing that – by definition – I did indeed go grocery shopping, so leave me alone.

For women who don't understand the nature of drug

addiction, their brains explain it the only way that makes sense: An affair.

I was having an affair, but it wasn't with a woman. It was with the drugs.

I kissed Elise goodbye at San Francisco International Airport and boarded a plane for Asia. From the moment I stepped off the plane in China, it was a disaster.

I was so broken by the time I arrived that it was only a matter of time before The Leviathan realized they'd made a colossal mistake in hiring me. Without speaking a word of Mandarin or having the faintest clue as to how the health care system in China worked, I learned how to get Percocet, Xanax, and Valium within 48 hours of hitting Red soil. It was surprisingly easy.

Drug addicts are problem solvers. There was a hospital on seemingly every corner in China, each one stocked with the meds I was after. All I had to do was identify the barriers between those drugs and me, observe how they operated, learn their habits, and exploit them. It's much easier than it sounds.

In China, I was purchasing seven to eight boxes of Percocet a day, each box containing ten tablets. I would get on the subway to go to work, having just spent $100 on pills at the hospital, and stand next to a Chinese factory worker, thinking, "I just spent more on pills than this guy makes in a month."

If there was any part of my soul that was clinging to life, this realization put it out of its misery.

Once I found out how to score Fentanyl in China, which took about two months, it was game over.

The Leviathan approached education from a corporate perspective, making the job really difficult to take seriously. Kids were dollar signs to them, and cramming as many small children into brightly colored rooms as possible was their number one objective. The quality of education was secondary. If English was your native language and you had a pulse, The Leviathan would hire you as a teacher, putting people in my position in precarious situations, since it was our job to try and motivate and maintain this unqualified, inexperienced teaching staff.

The Leviathan used company songs, with company characters, from company movies, to inundate children with the English language, knowing some of it was bound to stick because the songs were so fucking catchy. After class, they'd encourage kids to beg their parents to purchase over-priced Leviathan memorabilia and Leviathan toys from the front desk.

I cared about education, but not about the company's share-holders, and since the school was all about corporate profit, I mentally checked out and spent most of my time high.

One fine, smoggy morning, I awoke from a Xanax-Fentanyl-Percocet blackout and realized I was three days late for work. I panicked. I scored a small bucket of pills the previous Friday (payday), with the intention of staying passed out on my couch all weekend. By the time I came to, it was Thursday, and when I jumped up to rush to work, I immediately fell down, unable to put any weight on my right leg. Looking down, my ankle was swollen to the size of a softball.

What the fuck did you do, Jason. This is not good.

I had a vague recollection of going out and riding in a taxi, before coming home and falling down, smacking my face against the side of a chair. But that didn't explain what happened to my ankle.

Once again, my wallet and cell phone had been sacrificed to the Xanax gods.

I had no time to backtrack – I was three days late for work.

Making things worse, our school had an event planned at a local park that day, to recruit families and sell Leviathan English as a safe, nurturing environment where their child could learn the English language. I wasn't only three days late for work, but the work day was half over, meaning the event was well under way by the time I rolled up. I was still about 60% high, which isn't a great number to be at. I was high enough to be noticeable, but not high enough to not give a shit.

As I limped into the event, I tried to play it cool as if I had a great explanation as to why I was in the shape I was in. My khakis were wrinkled, my blue polo unwashed with an awful smell, and I hadn't shaved in five days. But still – the parents were looking at me, horrified, like some American monster who'd arrived to steal their children. They grasped their kids tightly, while my school's teachers kept their distance and stared, mouths open, trying to figure out just what in the fuck was going on.

"Sorry," I tried to explain, "I just got out of the hospital. I ate some bad food or something."

Honest to God. That was my excuse.

I wish I had an aerial shot of me on that day, because I'm pretty sure such a mass of people has never moved in such fluid unison as they did while trying to avoid me. Everywhere I went, they weren't. Some looked afraid, others looked entertained, but they all were in agreement that something very peculiar was afoot in the park that day.

After a half hour of being the personification of

persona non grata, I heard someone yelling from behind me.

"Jason! Jason! Jason, what are you doing? Jason!" It was Nick, the guy who hired me over the phone.

He snapped his fingers and pointed toward our school building, which was half a block away. I followed behind from a safe distance of twenty feet until we got to the school. I felt like a small child being reprimanded, when in reality I was an executive about to get a stern talking-to about The Leviathan and its "Brand."

I followed Nick into my office, where he slammed the door and just looked at me for what seemed like minutes. Silently, he stared through me, as his eyes traced from the top of my head to my shoes.

He was waiting for me to say something.

"Hey, Nick how's it going?" were the actual words that came out of my mouth.

"Jason," he barked out, and then fell silent again.

"Nick…" I replied.

"Jason, why is your hair blue?"

"Huh?"

"Your hair," he said, mouthing the words extra slow to establish an appropriately condescending tone. "Why is your hair blue?"

Fuck. My hair is blue?

I realized in my rush to leave my apartment, I never looked in the mirror.

"Well, Nick, you see… I was in the hospital. I think I ate something…"

Drug addicts may be great at storytelling, but we at least need time to prep. I was caught off guard.

"Jason, I'm going to ask you one more time. WHY-IS-YOUR-HAIR-BLUE?"

"Uhh... I... well... fuck Nick, I really don't know," I said, giving up.

"You don't know," he repeated. "You don't know why your hair is blue."

Silence.

Suddenly an idea came to me. "Oh, shit," I burst out, "the event! I dyed it for the event! I thought it would be good for the school, ya know? Fun, learning, English, you know... The Leviathan..."

"Jason, stop," Nick said, cutting me off.

He stared at me again.

"And your eye? Why do you have a black eye?"

Fuck. I have a black eye?

"My eye? Oh, that," I said, stumbling over my words. "You see, my eye... did I tell you I went to the hospital?"

"Did you get in a fight?" he asked, the question made more surreal by the giant cartoon Leviathan mural behind Nick watching this whole scene unfold.

"Actually... the eye, I think I can explain," quasi-honesty giving the faintest feeling of relief in this awkward conversation. "You see, I fell and hit my head on a chair..."

"And your leg?" he continued. "Why are you limping?"

"Ok, now the leg – well, technically it's my ankle – Ok, the leg I don't really know, but I think I hurt it in a taxi."

As I said the words out loud, hearing them made me laugh, making things far worse than they otherwise would have been.

"Jason, you think this is funny?"

"No, man, it's just..." I stuttered, trying to keep a straight face. I couldn't stop laughing because my life was just THAT fucking absurd. "I don't know, man, I mean, ok, seriously, I'm being serious now – I literally have no idea why my hair is blue." I did my best not to crack a smile, but couldn't help it. "I have no explanation for the blue hair. Or the black eye. Or the hurt leg – I mean ankle. Fuck." I wasn't sure why I threw that last "fuck" in there, but it happened.

He looked on, like he was going to burst out of his small, five-foot, frame. He was clean-shaven, wearing pressed khakis, an ironed blue Leviathan polo shirt, and here I was, 6'2, wrinkled to shit, just woke up out of a blackout with the beginnings of a beard, a black eye, blue hair, and a limp.

"That's all you can say, Jason? The F-word?"

This made me laugh harder, since Nick couldn't even bring himself to say the word "fuck" while dressed in his blue Leviathan uniform..

"Jason," he said, condescendingly, which pissed me off, "this is not OK. This is a problem. This company has a brand. The Leviathan has a brand, and…"

I cut him off and abruptly stopped laughing, immediately dead serious: "Then maybe you should have done a fucking background check on me, Nick. Shit, I'm fresh out of jail on drug charges. I need help, man. I'm a fucking mess, Nick. A goddamn mess, to my soul, man. Do you think I give a fuck about this company or its 'brand,' or this over-priced school or its under-qualified teaching staff? Do I really look like I'm in the type of condition to possibly give a fuck about any of this? Because I'll tell you right now, Nick, I couldn't possibly give less of a fuck about the brand, or you, or me, or life, or any of this shit, man. It's all a fucking joke. A really bad, fucked up joke, so yeah–forgive me for laughing at it, but at this point, that's about the only thing I can do to stop me from putting a fucking gun in my mouth."

Nick looked at me, emotionless. He turned around and

walked out of the room without saying a word. I went home and looked in the mirror to confirm that I did in fact have blue hair and a black eye.

My termination papers were in-hand the following day, along with a plane ticket home.

As I said before–I'm fairly certain The Leviathan doesn't do background checks.

"Damn, dude, you've been around," quipped my sponsor. "I've never met someone who's done so many 'walks of shame' through airport lobbies."

"Yeah, it was rough," I smiled. "I got thrown off of my flight from China for being intoxicated. They held me in the airport hospital until I was sober enough to sit."

"To sit?"

"Yeah!" I said, shaking my head. "You know it's bad when they determine you're too fucked up to sit down properly."

If you think about it, The Leviathan is the perfect employer for a drug addict. A company like The Leviathan is all about playing pretend. It's a suspension of disbelief, the removal of all things normal and mundane. Who better than drug addicts to create and maintain a fantasy, so grand that it becomes momentarily believable? The Leviathan cared so much about its brand, its image, that it forgot to confirm the existence of a solid foundation underneath it all. I looked the part on paper, and even in person. But just below the surface was a whole lot of damage.

"I was a mess," I told my sponsor. "I was out of places to run away to."

There's a reason the drug addict story is redundant, following the same, euphoric, pathetic, desperate, arc. When I hear an addict tell their story, I pretty much tune out the first half of it because it doesn't matter. Everything leading up to the getting clean is the same. Sure, the names, drugs of choice, locations – that's all unique. There might be, for example, a girl who prostituted herself for drugs after her man got sent away to prison for life. She's in a trailer, giving blowjobs to get enough heroin to not be sick. That story might be unique, and far different from mine on the surface. And those are the differences I would focus on in order to maintain my innocence, my "I'm not as bad as they are" mentality. Those are the differences I'd look at to rationalize my not needing a 12-step program, my not needing a sponsor, my not needing help. Truth is, I was no different than she was.

Think about it: Inside, that woman was so low, so deep into her addiction, that she did what she had to do to avoid withdrawal. There were drugs on one end, her on the other, and obstacles in between that she needed to overcome to get the high she needed to get well. How was that any different than the lengths I went to?

"Of all of this, what are you the most ashamed of?" asked my sponsor.

I thought long and hard about this. It was a great question. So many choices.

"That I didn't stop after my son was born."

CHAPTER 10.

NEVER ASK A GIRL HOW SHE GOT PREGNANT

"Jason," she said, holding a small, white stick in her hand as I stood at the edge of our bed. "I'm pregnant."

You should never ask a girl who tells you she's pregnant how she got pregnant.

"Wait, what? Pregnant? How'd that happen?" I asked.

Once again, you should never ask a girl who tells you she's pregnant how she got pregnant.

"What? How the fuck do you think it happened, asshole? What the fuck kind of question is that, you fucking asshole. You know what? Fuck you. Yeah, fuck you," adding in a few more curse words and physically attacking me with the small stick she just peed on. Shit was about to get real, real quick.

"Elise, hey, ok, stop, I'm sorry, ok, stop," as I tried to duck her wild swings at me. "I'm sorry, stop, just stop."

Like a boxer in the tenth round, she eventually punched herself tired. Placing her face in her palms and sitting down, Elise had the look of someone who made a really bad decision in life, while glaring at me sideways – the personification of that bad decision. Looking up, the emotional reality of the situation settling in, she let out a feeble "I'm… pregnant," before looking back down again.

Elise scraped me up off the curb when I landed in San Francisco from China, and I clung to her not because I loved her–I was incapable of loving her–but because I had nobody else. Thank god The Leviathan paid for my flight home, because no one in my life would have paid for that flight. My family and friends were done with me. They'd had it. But addicts are great at finding that one person, that one friend, that one family member who still has the slightest sympathetic nerve in their body, and clinging to them for dear life. They're called "enablers" for a reason. Without them, we'd hit bottom much, much sooner.

We find that one person, cling to them, manipulate them, exploit them, take advantage of every possible avenue they offer, and then the avenues they don't. We lie to them, rip them off, steal from them, drain them of whatever resources they might have, before finally pushing them to the point of not wanting to be around us, at which point we move on to the next victim.

Elise was my next victim.

I'd been home from China for only a few months when we got pregnant. Elise and I were two obviously broken people. I was fucked up beyond belief, and had been for the previous decade and a half. But let's be honest – there was something broken in Elise, too, for loving someone like me. There was something in her that wasn't right, because the average girl would have taken one look at the condition I was in when I got off the plane from China and decided right then and there to never, ever see me again.

Elise decided to move in with me.

The moment I heard, "Jason, I'm pregnant," my first thought was, "Ok, fuck, I have to get clean."

Ok, wait, this might be a good thing. Yeah, now I'll have a reason to stop doing drugs, a higher purpose. I'm going to be a dad – that'll fix me. Yeah, that's what I've been missing. Bringing a child into the middle of all this shit will be the cure I've been looking for.

If only it worked that way.

First month of pregnancy: "Ok, yeah, I need to get clean, but first I have to find a job, because we need health care coverage for the pregnancy, and I can't find a job if I'm going through withdrawal. What I'll do is find a job, and THEN kick. At work. 'Tomorrow me' has got this shit. It'll be fine."

Third month of pregnancy: "Ok, I got that job, but I can't kick just yet. My work will notice. I don't want to make a bad impression, do I? After all, they hired me high. They expect *that* guy. Plus, I hate my job, so the drugs make this mundane, monotonous career choice bearable. What I'll do is just 'taper down,' taking less and less, until I'm clean. But I'll do that next month. This month – the timing's just not right."

Sixth month of pregnancy: "Ok, I can't kick now, Elise needs me! She needs me to rub her feet, rub her back. She's sore. I mean, shit, she's pregnant with my son – how selfish would it be of me to be dope-sick, kicking, going through withdrawal, while she needs me by her side! Plus, what if something goes wrong and she needs to be rushed to the hospital? I can't be sick. No, I still have 3 more months to kick. What's the rush? I'll do it before the baby is born. I'm not an asshole like that."

Ninth month of pregnancy: "Ok, I just might be an asshole like that. The baby's coming any day now, I can't be sick. Besides, I just lost the job that was providing health care for my new family, yet another job I was fired from for getting high, which reminds me – she better have this baby fast, because they're going to cut off my coverage at the end of the month. Shit, how selfish of her to not have this baby yet. But I can't blame her because I didn't tell her I lost my job. I don't want to stress her out, so I just leave every morning, like I'm going to work, meet my dealer, spend the money I should be spending on the baby's arrival, and sit in my car all day, high, until it's time to go home."

It's showtime: "Ok, it's time. She's in labor, this baby's coming, and I'm still hooked on drugs."

Asshole.

Elise and I had a very unhealthy co-dependent relationship that I wouldn't recommend to anyone, but one in which many people in my situation end up. I was getting 240 Percocet per month from a doctor in Auburn, and supplementing the difference between what my doctor gave me and what I actually needed to not be sick by buying off the street. Elise didn't know about the street purchases. Every day Elise would set out my pills for the day and keep the bottle in her purse. The dynamic of our relationship – what should have been a partnership, equal ground, equal standing – was completely shattered. How can you have a healthy relationship when you are asking your spouse or partner for pills like a child? "No, Jason," she'd tell me, "you've already had all your pills for today." I'd counter: "Please, pretty please, can I just have one extra?" It was pathetic, and our relationship mirrored this dysfunction.

I'm not proud of the following story, but it happened.

And if nothing else, I want all of this shit to be real. So here you go.

Elise was horrified of needles. She hated needles, hated hospital beds, didn't care much for doctors. She was carrying my son, and for that alone, deserved my undivided, complete attention and care. Attention and care that I diverted elsewhere.

"Ok, Elise, in just a minute we're going to give you a spinal epidural," said the nurse, peeking his head in.

"Ok," replied Elise, the trepidation obvious.

"Jason," she asked, "I need you to hold my hand. I'm afraid."

"Yes, of course," I told her. "I'll be right here."

Out of the corner of my eye, I spotted her purse, lying next to the bed on the ground. I could just make out the top of my pill bottle.

"Yep," I continued, "I'll be right here," as I became obsessed with the bottle and compelled to do something about it, "right next to you the whole time."

Those pills were all I could think about. Here was Elise, about to have my child, and all I could think about were these fucking pills. It consumed every thought.

The nurse came in and it was a pretty big fucking needle. I didn't blame Elise for being afraid.

"Ok, Elise, I need you to sit up," said the nurse. I helped Elise sit up, like a gentleman, like a partner, like a father–but for none of these reasons. I helped Elise up because that was the direction away from the drugs I was about to steal from her purse.

"Let's swing her legs that way," said the nurse, nodding her head in my direction.

"No, let's go that way. There's more room," I replied, taking control over a situation I had no business taking control of, needing Elise to face away from her purse for this to work.

"Oh… Ok," said the nurse, confused but going along with it. Elise was oblivious to my manipulation because her thoughts were occupied by our child inside of her.

Swinging Elise's legs over the far side of the bed, I let go of her hand.

"Jason," she begged. "Come here. Where'd you go?"

"I have to sit down," I lied. "My back just cramped up."

"It's ok," said the nurse. "I'm here."

As the nurse placed a large needle into the mother of my child's spine, I knelt down, grabbed a handful of Percocet, and placed them into my back pocket. By the time I returned to Elise, the damage had been done. I wasn't there for her when she needed me, and I knew it. She knew it.

I actually felt this.

Elise lay down, the spinal epidural doing its job, and the nurse left the room.

Fucking. Hated. Myself.

By the time my son arrived, I was high enough to numb out that self-hatred. But I wasn't so high that I didn't feel an automatic connection to my child, and this sent me into mental chaos, turmoil, and anguish.

I assumed the love of my child would inspire me to get clean. What happened was actually the opposite. I loved my child so much that it made me hate myself just that much more, because I couldn't stop. Not even for him. Here was a love that I'd never felt before – the one thing that was able to penetrate my Novocain'd soul. I felt a true, honest, organic connection to my son the moment I laid eyes on him – and I couldn't stop. Not even for him.

And there was only one way to deal with this level of

self-hatred: Back in the dump truck, and pile on some self-medicating.

Worse, I added one more player into the dismal play that was my life – an innocent, unwitting, beautiful baby boy, who through no fault of his own, was born to a fuck-up father who couldn't stop doing drugs.

———

"Good luck trying to explain that to any non-addict," said my sponsor. "They're just not going to understand it."

"I love when they ask me, 'Jason, why don't you just stop?' as if that's some kind of deep shit, some knowledge that I never thought of. 'Oh shit, mom... that's a great idea! I never thought of that!'" I said, mockingly.

"But you can't blame them for not understanding," he said. "Our behavior is so absolutely bizarre to them. It's incomprehensible. I mean, listen to your story – a normal person would have quit a long time ago, yet here you are. You waited 16 years."

"Yeah," I agreed, "it's just frustrating. They just don't get it."

"Frustrating?" he asked, incredulous. "You think it's frustrating for you because your family and friends don't understand addiction? How frustrating do you think it is for them to sit there and watch you die a slow death while blaming any and everything around you? You want to talk about frustrating? You're not the victim here, man. We are not the victims. We are the perpetrators. Don't you ever get that twisted."

He was right. To call drug addiction a "victimless crime" is asinine. For addicts' families, the consuming nature of addiction is but a lesson in redundancy and heartbreak. It's feeling stupid for actually believing they'd get it this time around. It's wondering what they did wrong and how they could've stopped such a beautiful person from taking such an ugly path through life.

For the addict in denial, it's promises — lots and lots of empty promises. Nothing kills the soul more than failing, once again, like they said you would. Nothing annihilates your self-esteem more than using against your own will, possessed by an obsession to outrun a detox in $20 increments.

My soul was depleted, leaving death a suddenly viable option.

CHAPTER 11.

LIFE, DEATH, AND LIVING

"Jason, are you there?" I could hear Elise over the hospital phone that I was holding upside down because I had no idea where I was.

At least it wasn't a neighbor's shoe.

"Jason, I want you to hear me clearly," she said as I turned the phone right-side up. "Can you hear me?"

"Yeah, Elise, I'm here, go ahead."

I expected her to ask if I was ok, to tell me she was so sorry to hear that I overdosed at Thanksgiving dinner. Surely there was a sympathy reserve I had yet to tap into. I expected her to completely overlook the fact that my son was there, thankfully under the care of my dad, brother in-law and sister while I went into the garage to take a handful of Xanax, Percocet, and Methadone.

I even expected her not to wonder, "Wait a second... if you were high, then who drove the car with our child in it?"

My expectations were, shall we say, a little off-base.

"Jason," she said slowly, making sure I absorbed every syllable, "I want you to hear me. You...Will... Never... See.... Our... Son... Again... Never... Ever... Ever."

Brief pause:

"Do you understand what I just said?"

Of course I understood.

Once again, my dad drove me home from the hospital. I sat, quietly contemplating my demise as I stared off into the distance, my head resting against the passenger-side window. I didn't own a gun, so that was out of the question. My dad had a .22, but there would be no way I'd be able to get access to it without him knowing. I lived in a small town so jumping off a building was out of the question. I thought about the Foresthill Bridge, which would have certainly done the trick, but I was afraid of heights. Even in death, I was a coward. A handful of pills sounded ideal, but I'd probably just wake up again in the hospital, my dad driving me home afterward. I didn't want to keep wasting his gas.

My wrists. I'd cut my wrists.

My dad dropped me off at the house with a look that suggested he knew this might be the last time he ever saw me alive. I gave him a hug and told him this wasn't his fault. To my surprise, he responded back with: "I know." I suddenly realized my father was doing none of this out of guilt for my uncle's death. He was by my side because I was his son, and he my father. A bond that, for some fucked up reason, I couldn't use to get clean for my own son.

I had a Ziplock baggy in my room, hidden, with 30 Xanax and 30 Norco in it. I took 16 of the Norco and 3 Xanax, before snorting 2 more Xanax off of my glass coffee table, to prepare myself for dying. I still had drugs in my system from my overdose, so the Norco and Xanax put me in a comatose state, leaving me frozen, unable to move, able to do nothing but reflect on my life.

I stared at the ceiling. I was a failure. I had every opportunity in this world, experiences that most people can only dream about. I had it all. And thanks to drugs, I watched it all disintegrate into a fine, soft powder.

I lay on my couch for a week, in the dark. My apartment was filthy, baby toys scattered throughout. My son was 1 year old and I never had a chance to say goodbye.

It was probably better that way.

I hoped Elise would raise him with a real man, a man he could grow up thinking was his biological father. I didn't want him to know who I was. I hoped Elise would teach him nothing about me. I didn't want him to ever realize that, genetically, he was 50% fucked up because of me. It would be better for him to never know I existed.

I wondered if he'd remember me. There were so many nights, my love for him cutting through the numbed out emotions, when he and I would just look at each other and laugh. And play. He'd get the biggest smile when he saw me, his whole face lighting up, the way only a father's presence can inspire. I could see my eyes in him, his in mine. These moments – I prayed to a God that I was sure didn't exist, but was a total asshole by the way (drug addict rationale right there) – I prayed that he'd forget these moments and just start fresh with a better man than I could ever hope to be.

I ran hot water in the bathtub and went into the kitchen utility drawer. Inside was a small toolbox with screwdrivers, screws, nails, a small hammer. At the very bottom was a pack of razorblades, still in the plastic. I peeled the plastic back and took the blade that was sitting on top.

I took my shirt off but left my pants on, since I wasn't

sure exactly who would find me. Like my uncle, I went into the water in my jeans. I figured my dad would come by to check on me, which was a tragic choice on my part. But I wasn't like my uncle – I actually thought about who might find me dead, and was considerate enough to take that into account. Once again, drug addict rationale.

My father. The one who'd been there for me throughout the entire ordeal, the guy who took me to that first day of football practice, Hawaiian shirt and long hair. "What is up homeboys?" I was his pride and joy, the love of his life. And my selfish, self-centered, ego-maniacal-self decided that it would be he who found me, his baby boy, dead, wrists slashed, in a bathtub of water.

Drugs were not my problem, I realized. Life was my problem, which left me with a simple solution – end it.

Laying down I positioned myself with my head to the side of the chrome nozzle as it gushed out hot water. I turned off the water and began cutting. I quickly realized that I had no idea what I was doing. Cutting my wrists sounded easy, but in reality, I didn't know where to start. So I just sliced away. Finally convinced there was an adequate amount of blood leaving my body, I put my arms below the surface, immediately changing the color of the water in the tub to a light maroon. The darker the water got, the sleepier I became. Having taken my last Xanax, I closed my eyes and went to sleep, done with this world and all of its inequity.

Like I said in the beginning – it's depressing to wake up from a suicide attempt. Suicide brings with it the expectation of finality, so when I realized I was still alive, my first thought was, "Fuck, I can't even die right?"

The water was slightly warm, meaning I was out for at least an hour. The tub was full of blood, a much darker maroon than I fell asleep in. But my wrists had clotted up, refusing to hemorrhage, despite my intentions.

I sat up in the bathtub and cried.

Tears fell into bloody water while my brain raced. I wanted to climb out of my skin so badly, to leave this world, to just disappear. But I couldn't, and I felt the kind of frustration you feel when you're a child and don't quite understand emotions, that feeling of nowhere to go, nowhere to run, completely overwhelmed with sensations I'm not even sure science has identified yet. I screamed at the top of my lungs. I didn't scream words or thoughts or sentences – I just screamed. From the top of my lungs, as if I were trying to exude any leftover living that couldn't escape through my severed veins.

I couldn't live my life with drugs.

I couldn't live my life without drugs.

I couldn't die.

Suddenly, a mental picture of a name and phone number, reverse-negative colored, as clear as day, appeared right in front of me. It looked like a movie projector image, with my visual conscience playing the part of the screen. It was right in front of me. I saw it. As sure as I'm sitting here today, I saw it.

That phone number.

I'm not sure where it came from, where it originated, but it was there.

That phone number.

That guy.

A year earlier I played in a football game on Thanksgiving, and I saw him. I'd heard stories about him. He was only 3 years older than me, but was a lifetime more mature. Folsom Prison, California Youth Authority, and now had a wife, kids, career.

"Hey man," I asked him at the time, "I hear you sponsor?"

The game had just ended and he was drinking Gatorade while the rest of the guys drank beer.

"Yeah, I do. You need help?" he inquired.

"No, man," I lied, "it's not for me. But can I get your number? I have a friend…"

He saw through it, but acquiesced regardless.

"Sure, dude, whatever. Here you go."

"Thanks, I'll let him know," I said, pointlessly maintaining the charade.

That was the last time I saw him, or even thought about him.

Until now.

I pulled the number up, and sure enough, it was there, exactly like the projection I'd seen a minute before. After 3 rings, he answered.

"This is Bryon."

"Hey Bryon, I'm not sure if you remember me, but we met a year ago at the football game on Thanksgiving."

"Umm… no man, sorry. I don't. But what's up?"

"Do you still sponsor guys?"

"Yeah."

"I think I need a sponsor," I told him, defeated.

"Why do you think that?" I could hear his kids playing in the background.

"Because I can't die," I told him, describing my failed suicide attempt.

"Well, while I'm flattered your calling me falls somewhere past wanting to die, I need to know a few things."

"Ok."

"Are you willing to go to any lengths for your recovery? To beat this thing?"

"Yes." And I meant it.

"It's going to be the hardest thing you've ever done, that's the bad news."

I couldn't imagine anything more difficult than what I'd just experienced, but I figured I'd take his word for it.

"But the flip side is – it's probably the most beautiful, rewarding journey of self-discovery you could ever embark upon."

"So what do I need to do," I asked him.

"First thing you're going to have to do is stop thinking. Your thinking is all fucked up. When it comes to staying clean, you're an idiot. Always remember – the very best thinking you're capable of brought you to suicide in a bathtub. I need you to trust me. I'll never ask you to do anything my sponsor didn't ask me to do. But you're going to have to trust me."

"Ok."

"Now, tomorrow night I'm going to pick you up and we're going to talk. But between now and then, I want you to pray."

"But I don't believe in God," I told him.

"I don't really give a fuck what you believe. You're not calling the shots here," he said, point-blank. "Your beliefs got you in a bathtub of your own blood, so maybe you need to just shut the fuck up and listen for a change."

I couldn't remember the last time someone talked to me like this, but there was a strange sensation that came with it. It felt good to receive some sort of direction, making me realize I'd been floating around without direction for a long, long time.

"I don't care who you pray to," he explained. "God,

Jesus, Muhammad, Buddha, the universe, mother nature, the sun, the moon, I don't really give a shit. That's between you and whoever you pray to."

"I'm not sure I understand," I said, confused.

"That's because, like I said earlier, your thinking is fucked up. Stop thinking and just listen to me. If it doesn't work, that bathtub will still be waiting for you."

"Ok, what else?"

"That's it," he said. "Meet me at Starbucks on Elm Avenue tomorrow night at 6:00. Have a good night, and try not to feel so sorry for yourself that you do the most cowardly thing possible and leave your son without a father."

CLICK.

Did he just hang up on me?

I sat on my couch, blood drying on my arms, and thought for what seemed like hours, but in reality was probably minutes. I got onto my knees and closed my eyes.

This is stupid. What am I doing?

It felt silly. Praying? To what? To who?

I could hear Bryon's voice ringing in my ear. "Just shut the fuck up and listen."

"Ok, umm... God... hey," as I stumbled over what to say. "So... yeah, shit's kind of a mess right now. I, umm... I'm kind of scared. I tried to kill myself tonight, but I guess you already knew that. Yeah, and it didn't work." I stopped talking because I had no idea what was happening, but there was a wave of emotion coming that I didn't know what to do with. "I–can't–stop–I just can't. I've tried so many times, and I can't. And that scares me. This fucking thing has got me, man. Bad. It's like it has a hold of my soul and won't let go, no matter how hard I try." The more I talked, the more naturally it started flowing. "But I want to stop. I don't want to do this anymore. It's not fun anymore. Fuck, man, I just want to stop." This was the first time I'd ever felt that, the feeling of wanting to stop. I'd known I should stop, or felt like I should stop, but never, EVER, had I truly wanted to be done. Until now.

"I don't want my son to see me like this," I explained, and as I did, I felt tears rolling down my cheek. "I want him to be proud of me, to look up to me, and that will never happen if I'm all fucked up like this." As I spoke, I began crying, emotions falling out of me. "But I can't stop. I need help. I've caused so much damage, so much shit, and I can't do this by myself. I need help," I cried. "I need help, please, I need help." The harder I prayed, the harder I cried, all alone in my dark apartment, the bathroom light the only light on in the entire house. "God, I almost left my son alone. He would have never known me." As that sentence finished, I couldn't hold it together anymore. I was a sobbing, wet, bloody, hyperventilating, mess. "I'm such a coward. God, please help me. Please, help me. I can't do this alone."

I'm not a religious person, and I don't know how shit works. I don't know who made what, when he or she or it made it, and I don't get wrapped up in religious debates or religious talk. But this wasn't a religious experience – it was a spiritual one. I felt something awaken inside me, something that I numbed out for so long, something I thought was dead. It was slight, but significant.

I was connecting to the belief that there was something greater than myself, and that was important, because for so long, I was the center of the universe. I was the God of my own world, and when it came crashing down, I reached for a life-raft.

I cried myself to sleep that night, half-solemn, half-relief.

I wanted to stop. I just needed to learn how.

———

"And here you are," said Bryon.

"Here I am."

"Do you understand how you have to take accountability for your actions, and stop blaming everybody around you? You did this. You're the cause of all this shit, which is hard, I know. Believe me, I know. But the good news is, if you're the problem, then you can find the solution."

"But what about shit that happened to us, that wasn't our fault. Shit that really fucked us up, through no fault of our own?" I asked him.

"You're talking about stuff from childhood?"

"Yes," I replied.

"It's all about perspective. I'm telling you right now, that everybody you have resentment toward, or that you hate, or that you blame – by taking accountability and shifting your perspective, you can process it. And if you process it, you can begin to heal."

"I don't know, man," I countered.

"No? Give me an example. Let's test out Jason's thinking, shall we?"

Bryon just looked on and without realizing it, was about to teach me to let go of something that cut my innocence in half at a young age, creating a dividing line of BEFORE and AFTER.

CHAPTER 12.

THE THINGS MEN AREN'T SUPPOSED TO TALK ABOUT

Spring Valley, California, sometime in the mid 1980s. My best friend Justin and I were inseparable. We rode bikes, caught bugs, went fishing, played sports. He lived across the street from me and he was the closest thing I had to a brother. He was my first best friend.

He had a brother named Gabe, who was five years older than us. I didn't pay too much attention to Gabe. He was older and did whatever it was that older kids did, which was different than the things Justin and I did. There was no reason for him to be a part of my life.

Until the day he changed all of that.

Justin's parents were gone, and we were playing with toys in the living room. I'd brought over my He-Man Battle Cat and Castle of Grayskull. Together with Justin's He-Man toys, we had the whole team assembled to defend the realm of Eternia from Skeletor.

Except we were missing Skeletor.

"Where's Skeletor?" I asked. It was strange because that was the one action-figure we'd always argue over. It was always there.

Justin just looked down at the carpet, a defeated glance noticeable even to a fellow 6 year old.

There were two bedrooms attached to the living room, one of them being Gabe's. The door to the left was closed, but Gabe's door was slightly open. Skeletor stood just inside the room, waiting for Justin and me to come get him.

"Don't go in there," Justin told me. "Just leave it there." I'd never seen him so serious before.

"But we need Skeletor," I protested. "For Snake Mountain."

"Jason," he begged. "Don't do it. Don't go in there. PLEASE."

I wasn't listening. I wanted that toy, and it was just over there. I stood up and walked toward the toy. I think I heard "Jason, don't!" but I can't be certain. As soon as I entered the bedroom, the door slammed. Gabe was standing off to the side of the doorway in a place nobody could see.

I was like a fly that had been caught in trap, a horrifically spun web with just the right bait.

Gabe was much bigger than I was. He placed his hands on my chest, fingers gripping my armpits, pushing me until I fell back into the open closet. On the way back, I accidentally kicked over Skeletor, who just looked away.

"What are you doing?" I asked, confused, scared. " Gabe, stop!"

I was surrounded by hanging jackets and T-shirts. I couldn't see anything. All I could feel was clothes pushing up against my face. Standing up I felt Gabe push me back one more time until I hit the back of the closet. It made a loud thumping sound.

"Gabe, get off of me," I begged. But he wasn't listening. He had a smile on his face as he looked at me.

"Just hold still," he said. "Watch this."

Reaching down, he unbuttoned my pants. I could feel him trying to reach his hand down, under my pants but above my underwear. I immediately panicked, pushing back as hard as I could and knocking down the rod of clothes, the closet door, and Gabe.

He fell onto his back, crushing Skeletor beneath him.

With my pants unbuttoned I ran out of the room. Justin looked at me, surprised I'd made it out so quickly. "Jason," he yelled as I buttoned my pants, still not sure what in the fuck had just happened. "RUN!"

This time I listened to him. We ran as fast as we could out of the house. I was faster than Justin, but he was running faster than me that day. He ran from that house with a passion and urgency I'd never seen. I'm certain he was trying to outrun more than just me on that day.

Running down the street, I could see my dad in front of our house working on his VW Bus. "Tell your dad," Justin begged me. "Tell your dad what happened!" As we got closer, my dad overheard our conversation.

"Tell me what?" He asked.

By the time we got to the VW Bus, we were both out of breath. I knelt over, hands on my knees, trying to catch my breath while I thought. I wanted to tell my dad what had happened. I swear to God I did. But I also felt embarrassed. Ashamed. I didn't understand sex or sexuality, but I knew what just happened was wrong. I could feel it.

Justin looked over at me, as if this were finally it. He wanted me to tell my dad so badly, I could see it in his face. This was not just a chance to tell what had happened to me, but could also stop whatever was happening to him. Justin looked at me, eyes wide open, part trepidation, part excitement, part relief.

All I had to do was tell my dad what happened.

When I opened my mouth to speak, I planned on telling him. I had it all thought out:

Dad, Gabe tried to touch me. Gabe pushed me into the closet and tried to touch me. I think he's doing this to Justin too. Dad, Justin's scared. I'm scared. Dad, help me. Dad, make me feel safe. Dad, I don't know how to describe it, but I feel different than I did before. Something has changed. Please, Dad, please make it stop. Something is wrong. I don't know the right words, but something is not right. Make what I'm feeling go away, Dad. Please.

That is what I wanted to say. Instead:

"Gabe hit me in the arm."

That's all that came out of my mouth.

My dad just chuckled to himself. "OK, well, just don't go over there for awhile. You guys go to our house and play." And just like that, he ducked his head under the hood and continued with whatever he was doing before.

As we inched away, my dad poked his head out one more time. "If you want, you guys can play He-Man in the living room."

I looked at Justin and he looked at me. Nothing needed to be said.

"I don't play He-Man anymore," I told my dad.

"Oh," he responded, surprised. "Okay. Never mind."

———

"So what about that?" I asked Bryon, like a petulant child, with a "gotcha" smirk.

It was crazy because everything Bryon and I had done all day, all of the healing, the reflection, the getting shit off of my chest – I was still trying to find a flaw with his method, a loophole to prove the whole thing was bullshit.

I wasn't used to this. Men weren't supposed to talk about these things, things like molestation, sexual abuse. Sure, I could tell him all about drug overdoses, blackouts, fucking Canadians – that was easy. But child molestation was just one of those things men aren't supposed to talk about. Especially not with other men. Men were supposed to just suck it up, stuff it deep down, deal with it on their own. Men weren't supposed to reach out for help. Men weren't supposed to hurt or feel or cry.

Society had taught me each of these things, and it was about to kill me.

"What is your part?" he asked me, point blank.

I just looked at him. Silently. The question seemed ridiculous.

"My part? I was a fucking kid. I had no part."

"You're right," he stated. "What happened was fucked up and it wasn't your fault. But I'm not asking you what WAS your part. I'm asking you what IS your part. Your part in holding onto this resentment. Not your FAULT. Your PART."

"I don't understand," I said, confused.

"Look, as a 6-year-old boy, what happened is sad. It's fucked up. There's no doubt about that. But you're not a 6-year-old boy anymore. You're a 33-year-old man. So let's change the perspective."

What he said hit me in the chest, and he knew it.

"I'll be back," he said, standing up. "Think about that for a minute."

For 27 years, whenever I thought about that day, I thought

about it from the perspective of 6-year-old boy. Through the lens of a first-grader. Never had I once allowed myself to see it from the outside, from adulthood. I'd never even thought about adjusting my perspective. And suddenly, when given the direction to do so, everything began to change.

As a 6-year-old, Gabe was much older. Closer to an adult than to me. That's how I had always viewed him. Bigger, older, grown. But now, from this perspective, I realized that Gabe was only 11 years old.

Holy shit. He was just a kid. An 11-year-old kid. That shit that he tried...that's a learned behavior. He learned it from someone...oh my God, somebody did that to him. Perhaps to the point where he saw it as normal.

This didn't excuse what he did. But I began to understand.

I had empathy, from the strangest of places. I empathized with what he must have been through, because he put me through it. I knew how bad he must have hurt, because he hurt me the same way.

As a child, I hated him. As an adult, I began to forgive him.

I also began to realize that Gabe wasn't even the person I hated most that day. I hated myself for not telling my dad, for not saving Justin. I felt like a coward, somebody who had an opportunity to do something and didn't. For so long, I hated myself to the core for not saying anything.

But looking at it as an adult, I saw myself as a little kid, running toward my dad. There was no "proper" way to handle that situation, no playbook to follow. I was just doing my best.

Holy shit. You were just a kid. You were scared. Confused. Ashamed. Ease up, man. You're judging yourself for what you did as a child by the standards of an adult. That's not fair. You have to let it go.

This didn't excuse what I failed to do. But I began to understand.

As a child, I hated myself. As an adult, I began to forgive myself.

I never realized how saturated in guilt and shame I was until I felt it evaporate. All at once, it just lifted off of me. All of the pain, the resentment, the hatred for both Gabe and myself... It was gone in an instant.

On cue I began bawling my eyes out. Crying like a baby. Not out of sadness, but rather of relief. I tried to hide my face in my hands, but my whole body shook. Tears poured out of my eyes and goosebumps traced across my arms and shoulders. I couldn't remember ever crying that hard, and as my sponsor walked back out onto the deck, he didn't say a word. He walked over next to me, put his arms around me, and hugged me.

Men aren't supposed to cry. Men aren't supposed to hug. Men aren't supposed to talk about shit like this. Yet after breaking every one of these rules, I felt a freedom from something I was holding on to since I was 6 years old.

That was enough for one day, for both of us. Bryon and I had been sitting on his deck for five hours, and I was officially gorging on Ruffles and onion dip. Walking back to my car, I was different than I was when I arrived. As I drove away from his house that day, I felt for the first time in recovery that I might actually be able to do it. Stay clean. I felt a change inside of me, the first of what would be many. Inside me, being the key. For so long, I'd induced feelings from the outside. With substances, but without substance.

Thus began my journey of self-repair, self-forgiveness, from the inside out.

CHAPTER 13.

THE GIFT OF LOSING EVERYTHING

Wreckage. Its cleanup can be intense and overwhelming for someone new in recovery. I did a lot of damage in my 16 years of addiction. I've lied, stolen, cheated, manipulated, half-truthed, fucked over, fucked under, fucked around. Each of these produced some very consequential results, and I'm not a huge fan of consequences. Essentially, making the wrongs in my life right goes against my nature.

Think about it.

I'm used to numb. I love numb. I never had a drug problem.

I'll repeat that: I NEVER HAD A DRUG PROBLEM.

I had a life problem. I had a Jason problem.

My problem was the world and my inability to deal with it, the real-life shit that people go through every day. I found a secret off ramp on the crazy highway that is the world, and I took it, parked, and nodded out for 16 years. This worked for a while. Until, like always, it didn't. While I sat nodding out at a rest stop, life kept going for everyone else. Once I made the choice to re-join the traffic jam, I had a lot to catch up on. The scenery, cars, people, all of it – they were all different now.

The problem is, my perspective is skewed. What's a big deal to my cohorts and me in recovery might not be a big deal to the outside world. You can go to a meeting and say that you're "45 days clean," and they'll clap, pat you on your back, tell you to keep it up. They realize that for a drug addict, 45 days is 45 consecutive 24-hour miracles. They get it. But if you run around "regular" society, telling them you've gone 45 days without drugs, they'll think, "45 days? Without using drugs? You're not supposed to use drugs you stupid motherfucker. What, you want a pat on the back for not doing what you're not supposed to do? You want me to congratulate you for running out of a burning building? That you set on fire? Shit, 45 days, get the fuck out of here. That's not even the time it takes to make 2 car payments."

Addicts seek instant gratification, so if we don't get it from the outside world – that pat on the back from "regular" society for staying clean – we get discouraged, and when we get discouraged, we don't know how to deal with it. So unless we connect with a group who does know how to deal with it and has dealt with it, it's a very tough road.

That's why, for me, I go to meetings.

Meetings are a trip. You see and hear some crazy shit–shit that makes my story sound boring. But it works. I hear someone that did the same dirt I did and realize I'm not alone, that someone else feels what I feel. And if they felt it, and didn't get high over it, maybe I can do the same.

I had to learn to see similarities in other people's experiences. Whereas before, I only saw the differences, today I'm able to see my story in theirs, their story in mine. I don't care what their drug of choice was, how they got money to support it, or how long they went to prison for. In their story, I see the desperation they felt, that total abandonment of any sort of social and internal principles, that total disregard for self and loss of will–THAT'S the same. THAT'S where we connect. On a level much deeper than the story itself. I've been where they've been, using drugs against my own will, my self-esteem and self-worth evaporating with the drive to get more and more because whatever you have is most definitely not enough. It's never enough. Ever.

If you read this and think, "Yeah, but that won't work for me," that's ok. It's not for everybody. But this is what works for me, and it's my story. I'm not trying to sell you anything. I'm just letting you know what I did.

Something else works for you? Cool. Go write a book about it.

In the time I've been clean, I've dealt with some heavy shit, and through it all, my only saving grace has been recognizing my own part in the disaster. I can absorb, process, and deal with what I've done. But like I said – it goes against my nature, so it's been a project.

I walked into custody mediation at 60 days clean. 60 days! That was a big fucking deal in my little world. I expected to walk in, tell the mediator I'm 60 days clean now, so if we could just forget about my recent overdose in front of my son, my recent suicide attempt, my 16 years of abusing drugs, and just move on, pretending like all that shit never happened, that'd be great.

It didn't happen that way. Mediation didn't go too well.

I left mediation infuriated. Supervised visits? Are you fucking serious? I have to have supervised visits, with some county-appointed lady overseeing my time with my son, a son who I was used to having 3 days a week on my own? Don't you realize I'm 60 days clean? Did I mention that already?

Like I said – my perspective was totally skewed, but I was unable to see it on my own.

I left mediation, slammed the door, got into my car and called Bryon, my sponsor.

"Hello."

"Hey man, you busy?" I asked, voice raised.

"No, just working, what's up? How did mediation go?"

"Dude, fuck mediation! Fuck the mediator! This whole system is sexist. They just screw over dads, dads like me who are trying to see their kid. They're making me get supervised visits! It's so wrong, so fucking wrong. Man, I don't want to do this. This is bullshit. I can't believe they're doing this to me."

On and on and on I droned, the poor, innocent victim.

After ranting I heard Bryon laughing on the other end of the phone.

"Man, you're funny."

"Huh?"

"I said you're funny," he continued, "and I wish I had a tape recorder to record this bullshit so I could play it for you in a year so you could hear what a whiny little bitch you sound like right now. You're the victim? How about your son? How about the fact that you did something to get the state of California to step in to protect HIM from YOU? How did you get into this position? How did you put yourself in a situation where mediation is even involved in the first place? How did that happen? Did mediation just see you and your son at the park one day and say, 'Hey, they look happy. Let's fuck with them?' Bullshit. YOU put yourself into this situation. YOU did this. YOU are the reason mediation is even required. YOU are the reason supervised visits are now a part of the picture. YOU did this, not Elise. Not the mediator. Not the courts. YOU did this. And believe it or not, that's actually good news. Because you can work on you. You can fix you. I suggest you get busy."

CLICK.

Did he just hang up on me again?

He was right, demonstrating why I needed someone like him in my life, another man who could straighten out my way of thinking. Had I called my mom, she would've co-signed my bullshit because that's why moms do. "Yeah, dear, you're right, it's so wrong, poor you, the system is bad, I'm sorry."

I didn't need that. I needed some truth.

A funny thing happened. I wanted custody now, not later. I wanted to pretend all of my dirt was in the past, and should be left there, to never be spoken of again. I wanted instant gratification. But I played their game. I did my supervised visits, with some lady looking over my shoulder, observing my parenting skills. After a few months, Elise agreed to let me have my son at a local church, with the pastor checking on us here and there while we occupied the playground. After a few months of that, she agreed to let me have him at my house during the day. After a few more months, I got him on weekends.

Add these months up, and "Jason – you will never, ever see your son again" has become "Jason, I'm dropping him off on Thursday, picking him up Sunday."

Had I not gone through the supervised visits – church visitation – only during the day progression of custody, I would have never truly appreciated and cherished the days and nights I now spend with my son. I took that shit for granted before. Today, when I lay down with him for bed, read him a book, make him dinner–I know that I earned that shit and I cherish every second.

It took me losing everything to appreciate anything.

That self-esteem that degenerated into the crumbs for 16 years slowly began to rebuild by simply doing the right thing. It's taken its sweet ass time, but it's happened.

Today, I have a very healthy relationship with my son's mom. I will always owe her a tremendous debt of gratitude for protecting my son from me when I was in my active addiction. It's taken time to arrive at that perspective, but today, that's where I sit.

At 90 days clean, I met my brother in-law for lunch. We'd never gotten along. He recognized my addiction early on, and being the manipulator I am, I convinced my family that he was crazy, jealous, envious, whatever bullshit I could come up with to deflect the attention from me onto him. His home was the one in which I overdosed the previous Thanksgiving, in front of his son. As we sat down, I was nervous. I had no idea what to say, but I knew what not to say: "I'm sorry."

Addicts wear the shit out of that word, to the point where it becomes synonymous with "I fucked up again, can we just pretend it never happened." Our families, friends, co-workers, colleagues, are all sick of hearing us apologize. It's meaningless. There is nothing to it, a simple cop-out for whatever insane behavior we recently displayed.

"Look, man, I just wanted to sit down and talk to you," I told him as we sat outside of a grungy Mexican food joint.

"Go ahead," he said, looking skeptical.

"So… I know we haven't always gotten along, and that's on me. I haven't been a very good brother in-law to you, brother to your wife, uncle to your son. I've been fucked up, for a long, long time, and because you were able to see it early on, I lashed out at you. And that wasn't right. You're an amazing husband to my sister, an amazing father to my nephew. There are so many characteristics in you that I hope to one day have. And as long as I'm doing drugs, that's not possible. I know I've done a lot of wrong in your life. I've lied to you. I've stolen from you. Shit, I still owe you money for that plane ticket home after I overdosed in Nice. So much wrong, so many instances of unacceptable behavior that I forced you to watch. I forced you to watch me die, and it was wrong, and worse – I let the chaos of my life drift into yours, and that's not fair. I've done a lot of wrong, man. A lot. But I want you to know – I want to make it right. I want to make it right, all of this. And if I have to spend the rest of my life making that happen, I'll do it. You tell me how to make it right, and I will do it, because I love you and it's what you deserve."

The pause hung in the air, and he just looked at me. Finally, breaking the silence in half, he spoke.

"In the 18 years I've known you, that's the realest shit I've ever heard you say. I want to say thank you... I want to say that I accept your apology, but you didn't apologize, and that's good. Because if you said you were sorry, I was going to get up and leave. You asked me how you can make it right? I want you to keep doing whatever you're doing, because it's working. Don't stop, and I'm excited to see where you end up."

I felt an immediate release, something off of my chest that I had never realized was there. It was almost a natural high, the high of doing something right. The high of not being a fuck up. The high of surprising someone who expected the worst.

Finishing lunch, he gave me a hug, told me he loved me, and went back to work.

I got into my car and began my journey home, ready and willing to take on whatever came next.

CHAPTER 14.

MY LAST 10 DOLLARS

From his top bunk I could feel him trying to climb in and out of his non-existent sheets. They don't give you sheets in jail, the only real acceptable place where an adult can call a bunk-bed home.

This was my last piece of wreckage to clean up from my days of disintegrating into drug addiction, and walking into jail to turn myself in at two-years clean was surprisingly easy. I was just ready to be done with the dark cloud of courtrooms and lawyers that had occupied my mind and its thoughts for the previous few years.

One week. In and out. No problem.

I got a job as soon as I arrived to make the days pass quicker. I sliced bread. A shit-ton-of-bread. We made all of the bread for our facility, the RCCC, and the downtown Sacramento high-rise jail. A few thousand loaves a day, each one passing through my hands, through the slicer, bagged, placed in groups of five, stacked fourteen high.

Good times.

His name was Tyler and he was a heroin addict. He wasn't in for heroin, but his body didn't really give a shit what he was in for. All it knew was that it wanted heroin, he wasn't providing it, and it was going to make him pay. The brain can be a motherfucker when it wants to be. I know. Believe me, this I know.

And now I got to participate in his misery by being on the bunk beneath his while he went through withdrawal, feeling the frame shake every time his legs twitched. It really was a great metaphor for how addiction affects those around us, regardless of whether we choose to be a part of it or not. Here was this guy, going through a kick, and it was affecting me by keeping me awake. It made me wonder just how many people I forced to sit beneath my bunk.

I could picture him above me, sweating, yawning, sneezing, aching––the only thing keeping him from screaming being the brothers to our right who'd probably give him one warning: "Quit being a bitch," before whipping his ass for keeping them awake.

God, I didn't miss those days.

Morning finally came.

"How you feeling?" I asked, already knowing the answer but choosing to empathize.

"Like shit, man. This fucking sucks," he argued, as if I had any control over the situation.

"Come on man, walk with me," I said. "You need to sweat that shit out."

What drew me to Tyler was having been where he was. There's a certain connection addicts feel to one another, an empathy. Truth is, I felt bad for the kid. Kicking in jail sucks. I've been there. And if there's something I can do to make it suck a little less, then I'll do what I can.

Avoid the assumption of pure altruism. Helping Tyler ultimately helped me. I needed this. This was for me, he simply the product of me doing what I needed to do to stay clean. When my sponsor chose to sit on his deck and hear my story, he did that for himself. Hearing my story, all of my shit, kept him clean. That's the counter-intuitive nature of recovery. You help yourself by helping others, so I chose to help Tyler.

Tyler hopped off of the top bunk and followed me. It was our dorm's time for "yard," which was comprised of a baseball field, basketball court, handball court, and a spot for people to exercise. We got an hour every few days.

Our facility, the RCCC, was an "honor farm" that was, for all intents and purposes, the county's version of a small prison. There were no bars or what you'd typically picture a jail to look like. We were in dorms of about 150 people, and everything you did was with your particular dorm. Ours was Dormitory C. It's laid out like a military base, a tower hovering above us with armed guards just waiting for someone to do some dumb shit.

The dorms were segregated inside by race: Whites, blacks, Mexicans (two gangs: norteños and sureños), and the "others." That's really what they call themselves — they're made up of Asians, Islanders, and sometimes Russians (Russians can choose whether they're part of the whites or The Others. The Russians in our dorm associated with The Others).

Races are essentially unions in jail. It's not so much racism as it is protection. Each race has a leader, similar to a union rep, in the dorm. If you want to fight someone from another race, your leader goes to the leader of the race you want to fight, and they work out the details. It's all very orderly, in a chaotic sense. 99% of the time it keeps the peace. But when that 1% pops off, there's a race riot.

Tyler followed me out to the yard, hunched over as his spirit fought to return to normalcy after years of saturation in black-tar heroin.

"Dude, I don't belong here. This is bullshit, I need to get out. I didn't do anything wrong. I…"

I cut him off.

"Aye, I'm telling you right now you need to cool it with that 'I'm innocent' bullshit. Nobody here wants to hear that."

"But…"

"Stop, man. I'm only telling you because I don't want to see you get your ass beat in the shower. You can't be whining about anything here. People will give you a pass because they see you kicking, and most people had to kick when they got here. But you start with that 'I'm innocent' shit, they're not going to cut you any slack."

He looked down, finally realizing that he was in here until they decided to let him out, while I looked down, realizing I sounded like Bryon, my sponsor.

"How long did it take you?" he asked me.

That's the funny thing about drug addicts. We can always tell a fellow-addict, right down to the drug of choice.

"I had my final kick about two years ago," I said.

"Two years ago? Then why are you in here?" he asked, confused.

"Because two years and one week ago, I did something stupid. And now I'm paying for it," I explained.

"Heroin?" he asked.

"Naw. Fentanyl. Lots and lots of Fentanyl, with Xanax-bars sprinkled in for the occasional blackout."

He laughed.

"It took me about two weeks to kick, but that's

Fentanyl. It takes longer. You should be good in about three days," I said to him, lying, knowing it'd really take him about seven days. But like Forrest Gump's mamma said, *a little white lie never hurt no one.*

We walked around the entire Yard, stretching our legs, chatting. He explained how he was in for violating a restraining order placed against him by his ex.

"I just wanted to see my kid," he said.

Holy shit. I'm talking to me.

"Well," I said, "apparently your ex doesn't think your kid needs to see you."

"Yeah," he said, "it's fucked up."

"A judge seemed to agree with her..." That sentence hung in the air as we walked.

"Let's be real," I said, finally breaking the silence. "Your kid deserves a dad who's not shooting shit up his veins. It's probably best he doesn't see you right now."

He just walked, looking down at his pride and self-esteem as we sloshed through muddy grass. We passed the basketball courts, went around the handball courts, and started on our second lap.

"I mean," I continued, "I'm not trying to be a dick, but it isn't easy to get a judge to issue a restraining order when a child is involved. So there's some shit you're not telling me, and that's fine. I don't want to know. But you need to get your shit together before you can even think about being a real father."

It was almost like I was being tested on my recovery, a pop-quiz that came out of nowhere. I'd long ago stopped believing in coincidences.

Suddenly, over the loudspeaker, "Workers — report to the kitchen."

That was my cue.

"Come on, man, you're going to learn how to slice bread today," I told Tyler.

"No man," he begged, "I can't. I feel like shit."

"If you go back to the dorm and just lay in bed, this will be the longest day of your life," I said. "I need you to trust me."

He stopped, dead in his tracks, looked at the ground and started to cry.

Honest to God.

"Shit man, this isn't the place," I said to him, under my breath. "Come on."

I tried to usher him along, but he wouldn't budge. "Dude, I'm telling you, not here, not now. Man the fuck up and walk."

As I tried to move him, I remembered my failed suicide attempt, the night I screamed and cried and prayed. I knew precisely what he was feeling inside. That dark, damp, filthy room. Tyler's breakdown brought it all back, to the point where I could actually smell the room I was in.

Suddenly, one of the brothers on the basketball court saw him crying and started giving him shit.

"Hey, check out the white boy crying! You know where you're at homeboy?"

The basketball players circled up, mocking Tyler, who was in no shape to defend himself. Whether I liked it or not, I was going to have to defend this Tyler kid, a risk, since I wasn't about to get time added to my sentence for getting into a fight.

"Shit man, like you can talk. I heard you on the phone last night begging your girl to tell you who the guy in the background was," I yelled out, while everyone on the basketball court started laughing, clowning the guy who

I'm guessing wished he had kept his mouth shut. "This dude is kicking—at least he has an excuse! What's yours?"

It was true. The night before, the guy was yelling into the phone, "Just tell me who I hear in the background! Who is it? Baby, just tell me. I need to know."

There are no private conversations in jail. Hell, there isn't even privacy.

By now everyone was laughing at the guy, who shut his mouth and went back to playing basketball while the guards who'd taken a temporary interest in our conversation dispersed.

"Let's go," I snapped, getting frustrated. "We're going to the kitchen."

We worked in the kitchen for eight hours, slicing bread. It was mundane and monotonous, but it passed the time. Slicing bread is a two-man job. One person to grab it and run it through the slicer, the other person bags and stacks it. We talked about our kids, our addictions. We swapped horror stories, glory stories, drug stories. Our stories were identical, when I chose to see the similarities.

Tyler was actually a really good dude. He was a hard worker, and I got to see the real him emerge from the shell left behind by the heroin. Each day he got a little more healthy, a little more human.

He was funny. Really, really funny. One day, while we waited in our bunks for the guards to come do their count, we joked about how funny it'd be to bring our jail habits home. Take showers in flip-flops, sneak peanut butter sandwiches in our pant legs from the kitchen to the bedroom. Shit that's only funny if you've been to jail, I suppose. I laughed so hard and so did Tyler.

"Dude," said Tyler from the top bunk, "I can't remember

the last time I laughed. Like REALLY laughed, a real laugh. Thank you."

It's true. Laughter is a basic human reaction, not a learned behavior. In addiction we alter our nature so much that we can no longer function as human beings, losing basic, human emotions and behaviors. We become inhuman and do inhumane shit.

Tyler was going to be getting out two days after me. On my last night we talked about life, recovery, addiction. He said that he'd never met someone who was clean and not miserable until he met me, and that he felt like he could do it. Like, really do it. Stay clean. Put down the syringe. Maintain the person he was clean. Be a dad. All of it.

I saw in Tyler what I didn't want to become, and could very easily become if I chose to go back to the drugs. Watching someone kick, listening to their perspective, hearing stories about their victimization – I didn't want that, and seeing Tyler was a living, breathing reminder of who I did not want to return to.

My brain is tricky. As time goes on, that Tijuana jail cell gets less grimy, the kick gets less horrific. All of the horrors and tragedies and travesties that were a result of my actions – they get less bad. Seeing Tyler amplified the colors in the picture of my addiction that my brain tries its hardest to turn black and white.

"I'm gonna do this, man. I really am," he said, quite convincingly. "Thank you."

"Don't say it," I told him. "Just do it."

He acknowledged it with silence.

Tyler, like most addicts, had burned every bridge to any other human being in his life. When he got out, nobody would be picking him up. He'd get on the bus to downtown, where he'd be dropped off and left to fend for himself. I gave him my phone number and told him to call me if he wanted to hit up a meeting together.

The following morning: "Jason Smith — Roll It Up."

I was out. When they returned my personal belongings, I had a ten-dollar bill in my pocket. "What the hell am I going to do with ten dollars?" I wondered.

Reaching across the desk, I asked to put the ten dollars on Tyler's books for when he got out. I knew he didn't have a penny to his name when he got picked up, so I figured he could have lunch on me after he got dropped off downtown.

It was a Monday morning and I'd been home for exactly three days. You don't really appreciate the ability to be lazy, drink coffee, smoke a cigarette, and read the paper until that's taken away from you. I was soaking in the freedom.

Reading the paper online, I saw a headline that read "Man Overdoses in Bathroom." I knew it was Tyler before I even clicked the link.

"A Sacramento man was found dead in the bathroom of the Subway restaurant at xxx J Street early Sunday morning. Police believe it was an overdose due to paraphernalia found on the person, Tyler xxxxxxx, a recent-release from the RCCC facility."

I can't help but wonder if he tasted that taste prior to dying, that bitter taste. That bitter taste of dying.

EPILOGUE

Sitting on a park bench, I see him approaching. Scraggly hair, sucked up, needle tracks on his arms. Heroin. Fuck, another one. Heroin has infiltrated our streets and is destroying an entire generation. It's tragic, really.

"Hey man," I say as he sits down on. "Glad you made it."

"So, how long is this going to take?" he asks.

"As long as it takes."

Looking at the ground, he fidgets, playing with his shoelaces, refusing to make eye contact.

"I'm not sure what you want me to say," he says, in a very familiar tone.

"You got some shit inside of you that you need to get out," I tell him.

"Why should I tell you?" he asked, suspiciously.

It made me laugh. Déjà vu.

"Because if you don't, there's a good chance you're going to die."

I could see the wheels turning in his mind as he faced that crossroads we all face, addicts and non-addicts alike, when it's time to take either the easy road, or right road. This decision transcends addiction, and most of us will choose the easy road, regardless of the inevitable consequences.

"Look, man," I said, "I'm here to help you because I've been through it. Everything you've done, I've done. Anything you've thought, I've thought. Give it a shot, and if it doesn't work, you can get a full refund on the misery and depravity your life has become."

He looked at me. Once upon a time, I threw my life away and wound up in a jail in Mexico, a hospital in Nice. I was running from jail in California and the Russian Mafia in Prague. I was the guy with blue hair and a black eye and didn't know it, scaring the shit out of Chinese kids. I was who he was: A guy who couldn't stop doing drugs, despite my life being destroyed from the inside out. I'd been to the same hell he'd been to, souvenir-scars and all. Our stories matched, but only the first half. I made it out. I made something of my life. I took my second chance and made the most of it. I owned a business, had a good looking wife and adorable kids. I was a productive member of society. He wanted what I had because he wanted to be who I was.

"Ok, so what do we do?" he asked.

"Why don't you start from the beginning," I said.

AFTERWORD & ACKNOWLEDGMENTS

I'll admit, writing a memoir at 35 years old seems a bit pretentious. Even to me, and I'm the guy who wrote it. But the way this whole thing came about happened in such a way that it leaves me with little doubt that in life there are no accidents and there are no coincidences. There simply *is*. All we have to do is figure out what to do with it.

I walked into a newspaper one day with an idea for a story, requesting a sit-down with the editor. I never thought they'd let me do it. With zero writing experience, outside of earning my history degree, and no background in journalism, that seemed a bit pretentious as well. But the story idea was a weight on my chest, a gnawing, nagging feeling that demanded attention. My goal walking in to the paper that day was to listen to them tell me why I wasn't qualified, thank me for my time – *nice try kid, but we're professionals* – and send me along with a newly-cleared conscience, knowing *hey, at least I tried*. But that editor gave me the opportunity to pitch and agreed that the story needed to be told, kicking off what would eventually become the writing career that launched this book. To that editor, Dennis Noone: From the bottom of my heart, thank you.

That story, *Heroin in the Foothills*, caught fire in my small town. I knew I was striking a nerve with the self-important city council folk when one of the council members questioned my statistics with the police chief (who confirmed my findings). That feeling... *that feeling*... the feeling of pissing off the right people, of shaking things up, of realizing that by sitting down and punching the keys, I could change things. I could dig and expose. I could upset. It gave me a drive for something that I hadn't felt since the drugs, still a compulsion, yet much more healthy and healing.

People like to minimize the intelligence of drug addicts, dismissing us as stupid. After all, if we aren't stupid, why do we continue to destroy our lives with drugs? What they fail to realize is that the decision to use while our world crumbles around us is not stupidity. It's insanity. It's insanity in its most obsessively-compulsive form. And maintaining an addiction for a single day requires more thought, planning, and on-your-feet problem solving than many "normal" people use in a month. The average person who doesn't understand addiction assumes it's a lack of intellect that causes us to do what we do. Shit, I was chewing Fentanyl patches in graduate school. Think about it. But this assumption – that we're stupid – has set for us a decidedly low bar. Society doesn't expect much from us, nor should they, really. It's not like we addicts and alcoholics have a track record of meeting anything resembling an expectation. Personally, I like this. Go ahead and underestimate me all day long. I love being the underdog.

But if you're willing to put your money on a long shot, let me know. I promise you'll be rewarded.

When I got clean there was this part of my brain

demanding attention. That part of my brain that used to do grimy, unfathomable shit to get high, that was on active duty 24-hours a day, always structuring, starting, planning, plotting the next fix – newly clean, that part of my brain was going bat-shit crazy. It was like a puppy, looking me in the eyes, letting me know it was going to completely fuck my house up if I didn't take him to the park and let him release some energy. It was then that I stumbled upon writing. Was it luck? Chance? Coincidence? Fate? I'm not sure. What I am sure of is that writing allowed me to wear the puppy out, leaving his ass too tired to do any damage once we got home.

Maintaining a drug habit as large as the one I maintained required a varied skill set. Take for example my time in China. When I got to China, I didn't speak the language, didn't understand the medical system, didn't know what medications they kept in stock, where or how they were dispensed, how doctors there prescribed. None of it. Did I just throw my arms up and say, "Oh well, can't get drugs. It's too complicated?"

Fuck no. I'm a drug addict. I figured it out. On my second day. I had drugs before I had a place to live, priorities intact as ever.

I don't tell this story to brag. Believe me, that's nothing to be proud of. I tell it because it tells all you need to know about the mind of a drug addict. We are problem solvers to our core. When our dealer didn't pick up the phone and we were faced with a day of being dope sick, we found a way around the problem. When we didn't have money to score, we figured shit out to make it all work. Car wouldn't start? We found a ride or walked. Right now, as I write this, I guarantee you there is some inmate in some prison in some state sitting in solitary confinement who has found a way to get drugs into his 6-by-8 cell. And when we get clean those skills don't disappear. They're still there, alive and well. And that's an advantage we, as addicts, have over non-addicts and non-alcoholics. We can use these skills – the same exact skills we used to destroy our communities by perpetuating a drug trade – for something positive in the community. Something positive in the world. But it's up to us to find what will drive us. Motivate us. And that requires action on our part.

I want to say thank you to my cousin Trevor Hammond for turning me onto a website called Medium. I reached out to Trevor because I had no idea what to do with this newfound passion I'd discovered for writing. I had just written *Heroin in the Foothills* and wanted to keep the momentum going. I didn't want to stop. He told me about this website called Medium where you could write something, post it, and if people liked it, they'd share it. If enough people liked it, various online collections would come calling, sometimes offering money for stories. So I gave it a shot. And within two months, I went from a guy who'd never written to a guy with tens of thousands of people reading his stuff.

Greg Gueldner, thank you for being my biggest supporter over at Medium. At times your belief in my writing ability carried me through bouts of self-doubt and insecurity. You've been invaluable.

My writings at Medium caught a lot of attention. As in hundreds of thousands of people viewing my stories, which for a guy like me – newly clean, new writer, etc. – was just crazy. It all happened really quickly, and for whatever reason, people liked reading these stories, some of which made this book. Those stories caught the attention of Thought Catalog, the publisher of this book. Mink Choi at Thought Catalog Books – thank you. You worked with me and I know I wasn't easy. I was stubborn or I was insecure or I was needy – and you handled all of it. You made this whole thing happen, and I'll never forget that. Thank you.

I spoke up at a 12-step meeting for narcotics once, early in my recovery, about wanting to hide from my friends and family because I was ashamed of all the shit you just read about. After the meeting someone approached me and said, "You know, you forced your friends and family to watch you die in your addiction. It'd be a shame to rob them of getting to see you come to life." And they walked off, never to be seen again. This is why I love meetings. I heard what I needed to hear at precisely the moment I needed to hear it. Mom, dad, Windy, Jason, thank you for sticking by me and never giving up on the concept of second chances. I hope I can make you proud.

Matt & Joey – you guys never quit on me. Thank you.

Bryon & Brandon – thank you for always keeping shit real, putting me in my place, keeping me in check, and allowing me to grow by watching you grow. There is no book if there is no recovery, and there is no recovery if there weren't you guys. Thank you.

Liz – Thank you for being such an amazing mom to our son. We are both blessed to have you in our lives.

And finally, thank you to my wife Megan. You're the person who keeps me sane, whose strength makes it possible for me to do what I do. When I dive into the dark places that I sometimes write about, you're the light waiting for me at the surface. I couldn't do any of this without you. You're out of my league, but I'm totally ok with that.

ABOUT THE AUTHOR

Photo Credit: © Talia Marie Photography

Jason Smith is a graduate of the University of California, Davis, whose work has been published extensively in both online and print media. His eclectic style ranges from personal essays to investigative reporting, drawing on his own personal travels and experiences.

Jason currently lives in northern California with his wife Megan and two children, Jaden and Isabella. Visit his website: www.authorjasonsmith.com and find him on Twitter @mrjayzone.

Printed in Great Britain
by Amazon

28236955R00119